Frankston Library Service

Please return items by the date printed on your loans docket.
To renew loans by phone, quote your library card number or go to
http://library.frankston.vic.gov.au. Overdue items cannot be renewed
Fees are charged for items returned late.

FRANKSTON LIBRARY
60 Playne Street
Frankston 3199
Victoria Australia
Tel: (03) 9784 1020
Fax: (03) 9783 2616
TTY (03) 9784 1707

CARRUM DOWNS LIBRARY
203 Lyrebird Drive
Carrum Downs 3201
Victoria Australia
Tel: (03) 9782 0418
Fax: (03) 9782 0187
TTY (03) 9782 6871

J.M.W. TURNER

Also in Peter Ackroyd's BRIEF LIVES
Chaucer

Also by Peter Ackroyd
FICTION
The Great Fire of London
The Last Testament of Oscar Wilde
Hawksmoor
Chatterton
First Light
English Music
The House of Doctor Dee
Dan Leno and the Limehouse Golem
Milton in America
The Plato Papers
The Clerkenwell Tales
The Lambs of London

NON FICTION
London: The Biography
Albion: The Origins of the English Imagination
The Collection: Journalism, Reviews, Essays,
Short Stories, Lectures
edited by Thomas Wright

BIOGRAPHY
Ezra Pound and his World
T. S. Eliot
Dickens
Blake
The Life of Thomas More

J.M.W. Turner

PETER ACKROYD
BRIEF LIVES

Chatto & Windus
LONDON

FRANKSTON LIBRARY SERVICE

759.2 TUR
240490
18414881
[BIOG]

Published by Chatto & Windus 2005

2 4 6 8 10 9 7 5 3 1

Copyright © Peter Ackroyd 2005

Peter Ackroyd has asserted his right under the Copyright, Designs
and Patents Act 1988 to be identified as the author of this work

This book is sold subject to the condition that it shall not, by way of trade
or otherwise, be lent, resold, hired out, or otherwise circulated without
the publisher's prior consent in any form of binding or cover other than
that in which it is published and without a similar condition including this
condition being imposed on the subsequent purchaser

First published in Great Britain in 2005 by
Chatto & Windus
Random House, 20 Vauxhall Bridge Road,
London SW1V 2SA

Random House Australia (Pty) Limited
20 Alfred Street, Milsons Point, Sydney,
New South Wales 2061, Australia

Random House New Zealand Limited
18 Poland Road, Glenfield,
Auckland 10, New Zealand

Random House (Pty) Limited
Endulini, 5A Jubilee Road, Parktown 2193, South Africa

The Random House Group Limited Reg. No. 954009
www.randomhouse.co.uk

A CIP catalogue record for this book is available from the British Library

ISBN 0 7011 6987 7

Papers used by Random House are natural, recyclable products made
from wood grown in sustainable forests; the manufacturing processes
conform to the environmental regulations of the country of origin

Typeset in Galliard by SX Composing DTP, Rayleigh, Essex
Printed and bound in Great Britain by
Clays Ltd, St Ives Plc

Contents

List of Illustrations

11 J. Linnell: studies made during Turner's lecture on perspective, 27 Jan. 1812; pencil. Tate Gallery
12 G. Jones: *Turner's Gallery: the artist showing his work,* c. 1852; oil. Ashmolean Museum, Oxford
13 R. Doyle: *Turner painting one of his pictures,* from *The Almanack of the Month,* June 1846. National Portrait Gallery
14 George Richmond: *Portrait of Ruskin,* 1843; photogravure after a lost water-colour. Ruskin Library, University of Lancaster
15 John Ruskin: *Turner . . . dressed for a visit to the Royal Academy,* c. 1840; silhouette. Royal Academy

Colour Section

1 *Self-portrait,* c. 1799; oil. Turner Collection, Tate Gallery
2 S.W. Parrott: *Turner on Varnishing Day at the Royal Academy,* c. 1846; oil on panel. Sheffield City Art Galleries (Ruskin Gallery)
3 *Snow Storm: Hannibal and his Army Crossing the Alps,* 1812; oil. Turner Collection, Tate Gallery
4 *Frosty Morning,* 1813; oil. Turner Collection, Tate Gallery
5 *Dido Building Carthage, or the rise of the Carthaginian Empire* (detail), 1815; oil. National Gallery
6 *Petworth Park,* c. 1828; oil. Turner Collection, Tate Gallery
7 *Calais Pier, An English Packet Arriving,* 1803; oil. National Gallery
8 *Messieurs les Voyageurs,* 1829; water-colour and body-

colour (gouache) with scraping out. BAL/British Museum

9 *Staffa, Fingal's Cave*, 1832; oil on canvas. © Yale Center for British Art, Paul Mellon Collection, USA/BAL.

10 *The Battle of Trafalgar*, 1824; oil. National Maritime Museum, Greenwich

11 *The Fighting Temeraire*, 1838; oil. National Gallery

Turner in the print room at the British Museum.

Chapter One
1775–1799

J oseph Mallord William Turner was a child of London. His father owned a barber's shop in Maiden Lane, off Covent Garden, having migrated to the city from a small town in Devon. His mother came from a line of London butchers. Turner himself appeared to all who knew him to be a quintessential citizen – short and stocky, energetic and pugnacious. His speech was recognisably that of a Cockney, and his language was the language of the streets.

He had another direct inheritance. His father was short, also, and his famous son was said to resemble him. According to a family friend William Turner was 'spare and muscular, with small blue eyes, parrot nose, projecting chin, fresh complexion'. His son boasted, if that is the word, the same nose and chin. The friend added that William Turner 'was more cheerful than his son, and had always a smile on his face'. His happy disposition no doubt assisted in the success of his barber's shop, where the most important duty was to please the customer, and in any case he seems to have been a proficient businessman. He passed on his economical habits to his son. 'Dad never praised me,' Turner once said, 'except for saving a shilling.' It was a lesson he recalled for the rest of his life.

Mary Turner was a considerably more difficult character.

She was prone to fits of violent temper, and in the end her rages became so uncontrollable that she was eventually consigned to an asylum. A lost portrait of her suggested 'a strong likeness to Turner about the nose and eyes . . . she stands erect, and looks masculine, not to say fierce'. Turner seems to have inherited something of his mother's temper, but it never passed beyond the boundaries of sanity.

His parents had married at Inigo Jones's church of St Paul's in Covent Garden in the summer of 1773 by means of a 'special licence', which suggests haste or circumspection. Two years later their first-born son entered the world by way of the family house at 21 Maiden Lane. The infant was baptised at the same church in Covent Garden, with his trinity of Christian names apparently being taken from his maternal grandfather and great-grandfather. Joseph Mallord William Turner's date of birth, 23 April 1775 – otherwise known as St George's Day – was shared with Shakespeare's traditional birthday. There was another omen. Four days after his birth, a phenomenon of 'three suns' was observed in the afternoon sky – a fitting prelude to the career of an artist who is supposed to have declared on his death-bed that 'the sun is god'.

It was a busy, and noisy, household. William Turner's shop was on the ground floor, where he could be seen busily lathering the genteel with his soft badger brush, and the basement next door was occupied by a cider cellar described euphemistically as a 'midnight concert room'. It is an interesting coincidence that 21 Maiden Lane had been used as an exhibition room by the Free Society of Artists, and then later as a school by the Incorporated Society of Artists of Great Britain. London is full of such fortuitous associations.

At a later date the Turners crossed the road to 26 Maiden Lane, where they lived on the north side. The sun would in any case have scarcely penetrated this narrow thoroughfare in the heart of what was even then known as the 'West End'.

It was a fashionable area filled with actors and painters and prostitutes. Covent Garden itself was notorious for its bagnios and brothels – it was called by one contemporary 'the great square of Venus' – and in their vicinity there were of course many taverns and gaming houses as well as expeditious thieves and pickpockets. If you wished for a quick education in the ways of the London streets, then Turner's neighbourhood was the place to come. It has often been observed that in Turner's sketches the children have alert and watchful faces; they have what was once called an 'old-fashioned' look. In one sketch he has added the notation, 'Children picking up Horse Dung, gathering Weeds'. These children were all around him.

In the area, there were respectable establishments vying for trade, among them jewellers, print-shops and wig-makers. It was also a distinctive venue for the fashionable theatre-goers of the day, bisected as it was by the Theatre Royal in Drury Lane and the Royal Opera House of Covent Garden. It was perhaps not coincidental that the young Turner earned part of his living as a scenic painter; theatricality was in the London air.

When Turner walked through the market of Covent Garden he seems to have been entranced by the energetic variety of its life and by the sheer spectacle of its multifarious colours. His great nineteenth-century interpreter, John

Ruskin, noted that 'he particularly enjoyed and looked for *litter*, like Covent Garden wreck after the market. His pictures are often full of it from side to side.' In Ruskin's company Turner once extolled 'that litter of stones' in his painting of an Alpine scene. In later life, too, he loved to paint oranges as if in some instinctive reversion to the market world of his childhood.

And then of course there was the Thames, a few yards south of his home in Maiden Lane. It was down a court, across the Strand, and then at the bottom of a riverside alley – no more than two or three minutes away. He has become known as the great painter of the Thames in all its moods and localities, and his first vision of it was by the dockside of London with the wharves and the barges, the cargo-boats and the wherries. It was a dirty and noisy marine world, where sea and city collided in an embrace like lovers. It was a world of trade and barter, but Turner also noticed the rush of the tide and the boats 'shooting' London Bridge when the ebb tide was at flood. He knew the sailors and the merchants, the labourers, and the 'mud-larks' searching for pickings along the dirty shore. It was his world. It was the landscape of his imagination. He lived by the Thames and eventually he died by the Thames. It was an inseparable part of his being.

London could be fatal as well as benign. At the age of five, in 1786, his younger sister died of some unknown ailment. All at once he acquired the solitariness and intensity that are often the characteristics of the only child. Three years later Turner himself was sent away from the city by his parents to the more salubrious atmosphere of Brentford by the Thames; it seems that he had suffered from 'a fit of sickness' and was therefore despatched to the care of his maternal uncle, John Marshall, who followed the family profession of butcher. Turner lived above the shop with his relatives, on the north side of the market square, and became thoroughly acquainted with the riverside about Brentford; his child-hood haunts of Putney and Twickenham, Kew and Hampton Court, all feature in his later work.

He was sent to the Brentford Free School in the High Street, where he acquired the rudiments of reading, writing and arithmetic to fit him for a trade. But he began to display his interest in another career altogether. He once claimed that he had amused himself, on the way to school, 'by drawing with a piece of chalk on the walls the figures of cocks and hens'. His aptitude for drawing did not go unrecognised for long, and it seems likely that his first employment as an artist was in hand-colouring the engravings in Henry Boswell's *The Antiquities of England and Wales*. In that solid volume he encountered pictures of cathedrals and abbeys, castles and monuments; his impression of them must have been particular and profound, since in later life he returned to many of the same subjects.

After a period in Brentford he was sent with friends of his uncle to the seaside town of Margate where he seems to have remained for several months. Once more he attended the local school but his real education took place outside the classroom, beside the open sea. He never ceased to be entranced by the world of the fishermen – their nets, their boats and their catch.

His earliest drawings, dating from 1787, are of conventional scenes. The twelve-year-old boy copied or adapted views of bridges and castles from engravings. His first sketches from nature rather than from art were taken at Oxford, to which neighbourhood his uncle had retired from the butcher's trade. Yet it also seems likely that in this period Turner returned to London. There are repeated references to the fact that his father pinned up Turner's sketches in his barber's shop, for sale at prices ranging from one shilling to three shillings. In this period William Turner is said to have remarked to one customer, the artist Thomas Stothard, that 'my son is going to be a painter'. He may have wanted advice or encouragement from the famous man, but his son had enough energy and determination of his own.

The young Turner also found work at an architect's practice that instilled in him a lifelong interest in, and knowledge of, that art. He once told a friend that 'if he could begin life again, he would rather be an architect than a painter'. In later life he even designed one of his own country retreats.

So for a short time he sketched and painted for Thomas Hardwick, a London architect who was working on the reconstruction of St Mary the Virgin church in north-east London and who was rebuilding part of Syon House in Isleworth. For four years, in fact, he was involved in architectural drawing as something of a speciality.

Turner's early training instilled in him a deep love and respect for human dwellings. He seems to enter the very stone and structure of the buildings that he represents with pen or brush, as if they had some deep life with which he could commune. In the same period he studied under another master, Thomas Malton, a perspective draughtsman and Covent Garden scene-painter. The general impression is of a young artist busily imbibing knowledge and practice from whatever quarter he could find.

It may have been Hardwick who recommended that the young Turner should apply to enter the Royal Academy School. There is a story that he approached William Turner and told him 'that the boy was too clever and too imaginative to be tied down to a severe science. He recommended him to be sent as a student to the Royal Academy . . .' This was the place for aspiring young artists, where Blake and Gillray, Stothard and Rowlandson, had already studied. Turner found a sponsor in an Academician, John Francis Rigaud, who had been shown the drawings exhibited in the barber's shop in Maiden Lane. So the young artist began the first stages of his career drawing, as a 'probationer', in the surroundings of Somerset House. He worked in the Antique School, or Plaster Academy, where he was asked to produce a technically exact portrait of an antique figure.

His work was deemed acceptable and he was enrolled as a student. He was a model pupil (if the pun can be allowed) and for the next two and a half years he worked among plaster casts and broken statuary, where he drew what lay around him, including the body of the Faun and the fingers of Apollo. No better training could have been granted to him, since in these early years he learned the significance of line and volume. In the Academy there was no interest in teaching topographical or landscape painting. Turner was later to become the master of sea and sky, and while he was still a student he began to pursue these passions. Nevertheless an understanding of how to represent the human figure was an essential step in his training as an artist.

He also learned much from the now elderly president of the Royal Academy, Sir Joshua Reynolds. It seems that he was permitted into the great man's house in order to study his portraits. Turner may indeed have had ambitions himself to excel as a portrait painter, but there is little doubt that he was not suited by temperament for such a profession. So perhaps some good daemon or angel steered him away from an uncongenial pursuit. In the artist's house in Leicester Fields Turner would also have seen work by Rubens, and Poussin, and Rembrandt, their canvases haunting him like a passion. He once declared that he spent 'the happiest perhaps of my days' with Reynolds, and in later life Reynolds was the only English artist that Turner ever discussed.

In 1790 he exhibited his first water-colour. He was not quite fifteen, and yet already he manifests a firm sense of space and perspective. It was his first foray into a medium which he would dominate. The water-colour is of Lambeth Palace, but since the reverend pile is partially obscured by two friendly figures and a public house it is clear that the young Turner is more interested in the human than the divine world.

He was also occupied in less august surroundings, having been hired to assist the scenic artists at the Pantheon, a combined theatre and opera house in Oxford Street. Here, no doubt, he painted stormy seas and threatening skies for whatever melodrama was currently on offer. It was a way of earning badly needed income, to finance his more serious studies, but in any case he seems to have had a natural aptitude for theatrical painting. It must have been something of a disappointment, therefore, when a year after he had been enlisted in the service of the Pantheon it burnt down. Never at a loss, however, he turned up the next morning at the site of the smoking ruin and proceeded to sketch it. He neglected his figure work at the Academy for ten days as he worked up his conception. He was always fascinated by fire and by ruins; in this early work, the vigour and energy of his invention are already in evidence. In the following spring he exhibited his finished water-colour at the Royal Academy under the title *The Pantheon, the Morning after the Fire*. He would become more inventive with his titles in subsequent years.

He did not find his inspiration only in London. He seems to have been born for travel, and for the rest of his life he made journeys throughout Britain and Europe. In the early autumn of 1791, during one of the vacations granted by the Academy, he travelled west to Bristol. He stayed in that city with a friend of his father, John Narraway, and, as is the way with incipient geniuses, seems to have made a marked impression upon the Narraway family. One niece later recalled that the sixteen-year-old Turner was 'not like young people in general, he was very singular and very silent, seemed exclusively devoted to drawing, would not go into society' and 'had no faculty for friendship'. Here in miniature lie the later impressions of the mature Turner as brusque when not entirely taciturn.

He was asked to sketch a self-portrait by one of the Narraways but replied, 'It is no use taking such a little figure as mine, it will do my drawings an injury, people will say such a little fellow as this can never draw.' That has the ring of authentic speech, and emphasises Turner's extreme self-

Turner is said to have made this self-portrait while staying with John Narraway in Bristol in 1791. He was 16. The host resented the young guest's brusque manners, and hung the portrait on the stairs for 'he would not have the little rip in the drawing-room'.

consciousness. He could be shy and nervous, concealing his anxieties beneath the carapace of gruffness or rudeness.

Nevertheless, it seems he was persuaded as one self-portrait of this period has emerged, although its authenticity has been questioned; it shows a pretty young man with long curled hair and attired in fashionable dress. It reinforces the report that, in his youthful days, he was something of a dandy. And why should he not be? He wished to make an impression upon the world. That may be the reason also for the somewhat idealised self-portrait of 1799 (see colour section).

The niece also reported that he would 'sometimes go out sketching before breakfast, and sometimes before and after dinner'. He was at work all the time, in other words, and he was nicknamed by his hosts the 'prince of rocks' because of his constant clambering over the cliffs that overlooked the Avon. The sketchbook he took with him was filled with drawings of that riverscape. He was beginning to find his way as a topographical artist, and in the purlieus of the Avon he came upon evidence of the picturesque (to use the fashionable late eighteenth-century term) and intimations of the sublime. The water-colours he fashioned out of that experience were soon hanging on the walls of the Royal Academy.

When he returned to that school he soon graduated from Plaster Class to Life Class. He was permitted to draw only nude male models, who were set in graceful or demonstrative attitudes derived from the examples of the Old Masters. He remained in the Life Class from 1792 to 1799, a long apprenticeship in fashioning the human form. The results are perhaps seen to best advantage in the few so-called 'pornographic' sketches that were rescued from the misguided zealotry of his executors. He specialised in erotic female nudes, and even at the end of his life he was sketching female genitalia; most of them were burned after his death as a shocking example to the art lovers of the nation. Yet his more significant interests surely lay elsewhere. His drawings for the exhibitions of 1792 and immediately subsequent years are of ruined towers and monastery gates, of chapels and churches and abbeys. In 1793 he was awarded the 'Greater Silver Pallet' for landscape drawing, a silver medal donated by the Society for the Encouragement of Arts, Manufactures and Commerce. It was a sure sign that his immense abilities in that field were being noticed. It proved to be, in fact, the only prize he ever received.

Out of term-time he roamed abroad, looking for landscapes and monuments. He already had clients who would purchase his work, and periodicals that would publish it. One drawing was engraved, for example, in *The Copper-Plate Magazine*; it was a signal achievement for so young an artist, and alerted him quickly to the commercial possibilities of his gift. Over the next few years his work would appear in many illustrated magazines, introducing his name to the public. In 1792 he travelled to Wales and, in the following summer, he was ranging from Hereford to Worcester and Evesham. He also found the time and opportunity to visit Sussex and Kent, where the ancient towns of Rochester, Dover and Canterbury were available for artistic inspection. He regularly walked twenty-five miles a day, sketching quickly as he went; he carried all his effects bound up in a handkerchief at the end of a stick and, in this easy manner, he observed everything that passed above and around him.

In 1794 he was touring the Midland counties; he kept a list of interesting places, appending remarks such as 'fine' and 'romantic', as well as careful notation of the distances between them. He had with him two sketchbooks bound in calf, with brass clasps, that looked suitably professional. In the following year he returned to Wales, and then travelled southward to the Isle of Wight. His sketchbooks now had a title, 'Order'd Drawings'. He was working to the demands of his clients, whether private or professional. On the Isle of Wight, however, he was also indulging his private passion. He sketched the sea and the coastline, with the waves beating against the shore; he drew rocks and boats. The marine world enthralled him.

He returned to his parents' house in Maiden Lane where he used a 'painting-room' above his father's shop, but very soon after these drawing-tours he rented accommodation and work-space around the corner in Hand Court; his work was now becoming so extensive that he may well have needed the additional space but his mother's uncertain temper may also have contributed to his decision.

He went back to the Life Class of the Royal Academy, but in 1796 he embarked upon a new field of endeavour. In the exhibition of that year he placed his first oil-colour. It was entitled *Fishermen at Sea* and was a direct result of his sojourn on the Isle of Wight. He had already earned a reputation as a water-colourist but he seemed determined to emphasise his proficiency in all aspects of artistic achievement. He wished to express in oil what he had learned in water-colour. It is a highly atmospheric piece lit by the moon and by moonlight reflected in the water; Turner catches the desolation of the night as the boat is lifted upwards on the swell of the sea. The two reviews he received were favourable, and the painting sold for ten pounds.

He needed other sources of income, too, and during this period he was employed by Doctor Thomas Monro to copy certain water-colours in Monro's collection at Adelphi Terrace. A fellow artist of the same age, Thomas Girtin, drew the outlines while Turner was employed to wash in the light and shade with characteristic tints of blue and grey. Monro is believed to have thereby given both young artists a good education at his own expense, and Ruskin even called him Turner's 'true master'. One Academician noted that 'Dr Monro's house is like an Academy in the evening'. Turner was paid three shillings and sixpence for the evening's work, together with a free supper of oysters. But the work, which some have described as 'hack-work', was of material benefit to him. He acquired his mastery by intelligent copying of great originals. There is no better form of education. He is said to have learned in the process how to wipe out redundant colour with pieces of bread, a useful technique for any artist. When Turner was quizzed about this early employment he replied, acerbically, 'Well, and what could be better practice?' But the strain of work, by day and by night, seems materially to have affected his health. In the late autumn of 1796 he travelled to Brighton, where he might recuperate by the sea, and here he executed a few sketches.

In the following year he exhibited two oil-paintings at the Royal Academy; one of moonlight over the Thames and one of sunset over the sea and shore. The two burning orbs are seen in precise correspondence, lending ethereal warmth and numinous authority to the scenes. They were enough for the critic of the *Morning Post* to announce that the young artist possessed 'genius and judgement'. With great foresight he went on to say that 'he seems to view nature and her operations with a peculiar vision'. Another perspicacious visitor to the exhibition wrote in his diary that 'I am entirely unacquainted with the artist; but if he proceeds as he has begun, he cannot fail to become the first in his department'.

One of his water-colours in the same exhibition was declared by the *St James's Chronicle* to be 'equal to the best pictures of Rembrandt'. At the age of twenty-two Turner had become one of the foremost artists of his day.

He still did not feel himself to be financially secure – it is in fact arguable whether he ever did – and in this period he took in pupils. He gave lessons in drawing for five shillings an hour, but his classes were conducted in an informal manner. He told one contemporary that his practice was 'to make a drawing in the presence of his pupil and leave it for him to imitate'. He eventually tired of teaching, however; or, more likely, he no longer required the additional income. One of his pupils recalled Turner as 'eccentric, but kind and amusing'. The testimony of those who observed him at close hand tends to reinforce the impression of a friendly and cheerful man; it may temper the later legend of him as a crusty old curmudgeon.

In the year when he was being hailed as a young prodigy, he made his first visit to the north of England. He had been commissioned by *The Copper-Plate Magazine* to complete some drawings of Sheffield and Wakefield, but he took this opportunity to explore the wilder landscape of the north. He wanted to see the Lakes, also, and catch a glimpse of the glorious within his native shores. It is not entirely coincidental that, in the following year, Wordsworth and Coleridge would publish their combined venture, *Lyrical Ballads*, commonly seen as a harbinger of the movement known as Romanticism, which evinced the same pre-occupation with sublime landscape. Turner shared the same sea-change in taste and sensibility that launched the poetic achievements of the English Romantics, and so it is significant that he should have sketched and painted the landscapes where they also found their inspiration. As a result of this tour, also, he consolidated and extended both his range and reputation as an artist.

It was the longest painting expedition he had yet undertaken. He took with him two large leather-bound sketchbooks, and began work just a few miles from Derby. He went eastwards to Yorkshire, Durham and Northumberland, and then went on to the Lake District where he remained two weeks. He spent hours within churches, lovingly delineating the naves and the crypts. He hired boats to capture his subjects from a particular vantage. He was deeply studious and determined. In Yorkshire and Durham he visited most of the monuments of antiquity, the chapels and the abbeys, where his love of old stone is powerfully conveyed in images of church interiors and of church ruins. It is intriguing that much later in life he returned to the same site of these early endeavours, such as Kirkstall Abbey or Norham Castle. For the latter he had an especial fondness. One fellow coach traveller was surprised when Turner stood up and bowed as their vehicle passed the ruins of the castle; the by now old and venerable painter told him that, after he had completed a painting of Norham in his younger days, he had never wanted for work again. On these later trips he often painted the scene as it had been in his youth, ignoring any contemporary changes. His memory was still alive and powerful, investing the landscape and the buildings with a reality that lived beyond time. His final painting of Norham Castle, executed in the last years of his life, is irradiated by light and colour. The castle itself, which he had once drawn so delicately and distinctively, has become a luminous body. It has been transformed by the power of Turner's imagination.

In the Lake District he encountered the wildness of the crags and mountains. It was a great and inexhaustible subject. He was also entranced by all the effects of the mist and the water cloaking the landscape like some spiritual veil; he painted rain and rainbows, morning and evening light.

When he returned to London he had material for nine works that he exhibited the following year at the Royal Academy, as well as a number of private commissions. On viewing Turner's water-colour of Norham Castle, the critic of the *Whitehall Evening Post* deemed it 'a work upon which we could rivet our eyes for hours and not experience satiety'. Before the exhibition itself another Academician went to the gallery and 'found Turner there touching in his pictures – seemed modest and sensible'. In the same period another artist, John Hoppner, visited Turner in his studio in Hand Court and declared him to be a 'timid man afraid to venture'. He must have caught Turner in a most unusual mood. The significant fact is that from this time forward Turner became the subject of much comment. He had become worth knowing. He was, in fact, something of a celebrity.

That is why he had been commissioned by the Clarendon Press to complete some water-colours of Oxford, which could then be engraved for the university almanac. He had ambitions in another direction also. He wished to be elected as an Associate of the Royal Academy, even though he was below the stipulated age. He had many conversations with an *éminence grise* of the Academy, Joseph Farington, who assured him that he was 'certain' he would succeed. Farington also left recollections of what Turner said on this occasion. The aspiring young painter was not sure if he should still reside in the vicinity of Maiden Lane – 'He thought he might derive advantages from placing himself in a more respectable situation. He said, he had more commissions at present than he could execute and got more money than he expended.' By 'more respectable' he meant of a higher social class; now that he was making money, the surroundings of his early life were no longer suitable. Farington also visited Turner's studio and noted that 'the apartments to be sure, small and ill calculated for a painter'. So he had some reason to wish to leave.

In this year he made two visits to friends who have left a small store of reminiscences. In the spring of 1798 he visited the Reverend Robert Nixon of Foots Cray in Kent; Nixon had frequented the barber's shop in Maiden Lane, and had assisted the young Turner in the first steps of his career. Despite the professed beliefs of his host, Turner paid no great attention to matters of religion. Another guest at the parsonage recalled that 'he worshipped nature with all her beauties, but forgot God his Creator'. When the family party attended church on Sunday, a ritual that might seem obligatory in the household of the local parson, Turner remained 'shut up in the little study . . . diligently painting in water-colours'. His assiduity is only to be expected, but it is also clear that he had no interest at all in orthodox pieties. He loved ruined abbeys and churches, but he dismissed religion itself as of no importance. He was in effect something of a pagan.

The Nixon party embarked upon a sketching-trip through

the scenery of Kent. They dined at an inn one afternoon, and the Reverend Nixon called for wine. 'No,' Turner said, 'I can't stand that.' So no wine was provided. The reporter of this incident explained that he had demurred because of his 'love of money'. But, on this occasion at least, the charge of miserliness seems unfair. He may have wanted to stay alert – sketching, after all, was his life's work – and did not wish to mingle business with pleasure. The incident does, however, emphasise his single-mindedness. His 'love of money' did not preclude him from making a loan to a friend. In one of his sketchbooks is the notation, 'Lent Mr Nixon £2.12.6'.

He also paid a return visit to the Narraways, in Bristol, where it was remarked that 'he seemed an uneducated youth, desirous of nothing but improvement in his art. He was very difficult to understand, he would talk so little . . .' But this is characteristic. Artists are not, on the whole, intellectuals; they do not try to be particularly articulate and, when they do speak of their art, they do not do so in the terms of the critic or connoisseur. But that is not their job. They simply do it. It was also noted that in the evening he would 'sit quietly, apparently thinking, not occupied in drawing or reading'. No doubt he was thinking of the next day's painting.

On this visit he journeyed to Chepstow and Tintern, among other places, as well as to Aberystwyth and Denbigh. Some of his drawings and water-colours from this period are spattered with raindrops.

In London, at the beginning of November, he received the unwelcome news that he had against all expectation failed to be elected an Associate; but he did not have to wait long for that elevation and, in the meantime, he found comfort and consolation elsewhere. In the late 1790s he had become acquainted with the Danby family. John Danby was a composer of songs and Catholic masses who had for some years lived around the corner from the Turners in Covent Garden; he had also performed as an organist at the Pantheon, where Turner had worked as a scene-painter. In the small world of London such a connection can lead to a lifelong friendship. But life is not always so very long. John Danby died in the spring of 1798, leaving a young widow and four daughters.

At the time she was widowed, Sarah Danby was living in London, in Upper John Street. When we next hear of her, she is residing at a nearby address in Norton Street. She is in fact living with Turner. He must have approached Sarah Danby shortly after the death of her husband, and it is clear enough that his advances were reciprocated.

It will be seen, over the course of his life, that the artist had a particular fondness for widows. It may have just been coincidence but it does suggest some attraction to older or at least more mature women. He never married but preferred to cohabit in a looser fashion. This fear of commitment, if such it was, was no doubt connected with his intense privacy (and on occasions secrecy) as well as the individual nature of his visionary achievement. But it may also be related to the horror of his parents' marriage that he had seen at very close quarters. He always showed great affection for his father, and must have understood the misfortune of being tied to a woman who was straying further from the bounds of sanity. Turner's mother was subject to periodic fits of extreme rage, and the experience of the misery of madness within the family may have deterred him from any kind of formal matrimonial union.

It is not coincidence that Turner seemed always to need the protection of some surrogate family. Clara Wheeler, the daughter of one of Turner's friends, recalled how he would visit the house of her family as 'a haven of rest from many domestic trials too sacred to touch upon'. The young painter 'usually spent three or four evenings in every week at our fireside'. In his relationship with Sarah Danby and her children he may have been seeking an alternative family. Certainly, in later years, the Royal Academy assumed the comforting role of home.

In the year after the beginning of his relationship with Sarah Danby, Turner's mother was confined to a madhouse in Old Street. She would never be allowed into the world again. In the following year she was removed to Bethlehem Hospital, popularly known as 'Bethlem', where she died two years later amid the shrieks of the insane in the Incurable Ward.

It was a subject about which he chose never to talk. When someone mentioned his mother to him at a later date, his 'manner was full of majesty, accompanied by a diabolical look'. The reasons for that taciturnity are clear enough. It was always a subject too sensitive to discuss but, perhaps more significantly, he may have had some lurking fear of inherited madness. There would come a time, in fact, when Turner would himself be condemned as 'mad' by the more vociferous critics.

Chapter Two
1799–1802

In the new year, 1799, he was still very busily employed. He informed Farington, the Academician and indefatigable diarist, that 'he had 60 drawings now bespoke by different persons'; he was indeed now considered the best artist for topographical illustration, and was as a result much in demand. One collector offered him forty guineas for a water-colour of Caernarvon Castle. The celebrated dilettante, Sir William Beckford, asked him to paint his remarkable retreat, Fonthill Abbey in Wiltshire; Turner subsequently spent three weeks there.

At the Royal Academy exhibition in that year he confirmed his ambition, and his newly found fame, with the display of his first historical painting. History painting was, in this period, considered to be the pinnacle of artistic achievement, equivalent to epic in the field of literature. Any English artist worthy of the name had to master it. His own attempt, *The Battle of the Nile*, was of course concerned with contemporary history; it commemorated Nelson's victory in Egypt the year before, but it was no doubt executed in the grand manner used for sensational naval battles. It has since been lost.

Although he would continue to exhibit historical paintings, his artistic passion and instinct lay elsewhere. That is why, when he first saw the mythological landscapes of

Claude, he responded with great and uncharacteristic emotion. Claude Lorrain, the seventeenth-century artist, was justly celebrated for the clarity and harmony of his landscapes; he was also the first to include an image of the sun within his paintings, a shining talisman for Turner himself.

An art patron had asked the young Turner to see Claude's *Seaport with the Embarkation of the Queen of Sheba*, and a contemporary recalled that on viewing it for the first time 'Turner was awkward, agitated and burst into tears'. When he was asked the cause for this display of tender feeling, Turner replied, 'Because I shall never be able to paint anything like that picture.' This mid-seventeenth-century master-work, in all its luminous serenity, seemed to the young English painter to be quite beyond his grasp. When he saw two other of Claude's landscapes, at Beckford's house in Grosvenor Square, he is reported as saying that they 'seemed to be beyond the power of imitation'. Yet he sought for Claude's ethereal harmonies all his life. In later years he was in fact deemed comparable to the French artist, and indeed can still survive that comparison.

He travelled to Wales and Lancashire in 1799, in search of the sublime, and on his return to London was soon informed that he had been elected an Associate of the Royal Academy. This was the preparatory step towards becoming a full Academician, and immediately he joined a dining society known as the Academy Club. It cannot be said that, at this time of his life, Turner was averse to convivial company. As a further token of his enhanced status he had moved his studio from Hand Court and Maiden Lane to the more respectable quarter of Harley Street. In his new painting-rooms he had space to express his vision; he was also still close to Sarah Danby and her increasing family. He

George Dance's portrait of Turner. Drawn in March 1800, it marked Turner's recent election to the Royal Academy as an Associate at the age of 24.

never discussed his illegitimate children, two daughters named Evelina and Georgina, but he never disowned them. They spoke freely of their father, Turner, and he mentioned them in his will.

Soon after Turner's removal to Harley Street his father gave up Maiden Lane and joined him. With his wife confined in an asylum the old man would have been increasingly isolated without the help and encouragement of his son. William Turner then took on the role of Turner's general assistant, stretching and preparing canvases as well as writing letters on his son's behalf to various clients and patrons. He may also have acted as caretaker for the new studio. Or he may have shared the house in Norton Street with his son and Sarah Danby, walking to Harley Street for the day's work as the painter's factotum. For the remainder of his life he loved, and shared in, his son's success.

There is a story of Turner being invited to a grand dinner. When he hesitated in accepting, his father appeared at the door and exclaimed, 'Go, Billy, go! *The mutton needn't be cooked, Billy!*' It seems that William Turner worked for his son as housekeeper as well as painter's assistant, and no doubt wanted to avoid the unnecessary expense of dinner at home. Turner was in any case now a fashionable figure who might have expected many such invitations to dine out. A sketch by George Dance, executed in this period, gives the impression of a young man who is climbing to the topmost rung of his profession.

He was described by one contemporary as an 'odd little mortal', and by another as 'anything but nice looking'. He had bandy legs, and big feet. In later life he was variously compared to a sailor, a farmer and a coachman. No doubt because of his ruddy complexion, he was thought to resemble the captain of a steamboat or the pilot of a North Sea vessel. These marine similes would have met with his enthusiastic approval, however, since he always loved the sea and the things of the sea. His features were perhaps 'coarse' by the standards of the day, by which was meant that he did not really resemble a gentleman. But he was not a gentleman. He was a Cockney visionary, a true London type whose fraternity could be seen on the streets of the city. Someone once said that he was as ugly as a 'Guy', that creature of the bonfire parades, and in truth with his beaked nose he did look a little like Punch. He was also said to have hands that were 'not clean'. The reason is that he used his fingers to draw the paint across the canvas. There is a story of a visitor proclaiming himself to be an artist. Turner asked to see his hands and, when he looked at them, informed him that 'you are not an artist'. They were too pale.

In his new studio in Harley Street Turner completed the largest canvas he had yet undertaken, *The Fifth Plague of Egypt*; despite its biblical subject the effects of thunder and hail were taken from a storm he had recently witnessed in Wales. This was also the setting for the second oil painting he exhibited in 1800, *Dolbadern Castle*. We may see this as evidence of his twin preoccupations with historical painting and with landscape, except that both paintings are filled with gloomy majesty. In the succeeding year his *Dutch Boats in a Gale* was described by Benjamin West, the grandest historical painter of the day, as 'what Rembrandt thought of but could not do'.

With supporters such as this it was perhaps inevitable that Turner would be elected as a full Academician in February

The Cockney visionary in 1816. Turner looked a little like Mr
Punch, and this sketch by C.R. Leslie is doubtless a truer likeness
than the romanticised self-portrait of 1799 (see colour section).

1802. He seems to have been so elated by his achievement, however, that he succumbed to bravado. When informed that he should thank his fellows for voting on his behalf he replied that he 'would do nothing of the kind . . . Why thank a man for performing a simple duty?' He had become pre-eminent, easily the leading painter of his day, and he knew it. In the exhibition of that year he changed his name from 'W. Turner, A' into 'Joseph Mallord William Turner, RA'. He even became slightly pugnacious. He had an altercation with a respectable painter, Sir Francis Bourgeois, in which he suggested the older man's 'incompetency'. Bourgeois called him 'a little Reptile'. Turner replied that Bourgeois was then 'a great Reptile – with ill manners'.

On another occasion, shortly afterwards, he even rebuffed his old friend Farington; Farington and others had left a meeting of the Academy Council but, on their return, Turner had taken the chair 'and began instantly with a very angry countenance to call us to account for having left the Council . . . I replied to him sharply and told him of the impropriety of addressing us in such a manner.' Farington added that Turner's behaviour had already 'been cause of complaint to the whole Academy'. Turner was indeed being accused by other Academicians of presumption and arrogance. But since the public prints were describing his work hanging in the 1802 exhibition as displaying 'genius' and 'sublimity of conception' he had some reason for self-confidence. He was creating master-works of landscape and historical painting. He was being compared to Claude, Rembrandt and Gainsborough.

It is a sure sign of his worth that he was also being championed by the younger artists of the day. Where their elders considered him too 'extreme', too revolutionary, they believed him to be leading a necessary change in taste. He was in the forefront of the time, provoking criticism and jealousy while still moving ahead. Like many other artists of many other periods, he was accused of trying only to shock and to enrage the public. He wanted novelty for the sake of novelty. As one journal put it, 'A certain artist has so much debauched the taste of the young artists by the empirical novelty of his style of painting that a humorous critic gave him the title of over-*Turner*'.

Chapter Three
1802–1805

In the summer of 1802 the over-turner set off for his first journey outside England; in the middle of July, he travelled to Paris. That city did not then have the reputation for bohemian or 'artistic' life that it acquired in the late nineteenth and early twentieth centuries – Italy was still considered the natural home for art and artists – and, for Turner, France was only the first stage of a journey to the mountains of Switzerland. He crossed the Channel in a packet-boat, from Dover to Calais; during a severe storm he found himself clambering into a small boat near the entrance to Calais Harbour, almost swamped by waves. But what more appropriate entry for a marine painter who loved the turbulent sea? As soon as he reached the pier he took out his sketchbook and drew the scene.

When he arrived in Paris he hired a cabriolet and set off for Switzerland. There he revelled in the valleys and the mountains. He sketched Mont Blanc and the Mer de Glace; he crossed the great St Bernard Pass; he visited the Reichenbach Falls and the eighty-foot waterfall at Schaffhausen; he went along the St Gothard Pass as far as the Devil's Bridge. He was observing all the effects of the mighty and the sublime, finding amongst this stupendous scenery visions of the work he would accomplish. He told Farington later that the 'fragments and precipices [were] very romantic and strikingly grand'. He made four hundred sketches during the course of this journey, working quickly on the spot to create mass and outline.

On his return to Paris he made his pilgrimage to the Louvre, where he closely studied the works of Titian and of Poussin, Raphael and Correggio. He was not in a state of permanent rapture. He was disappointed by Rembrandt and disapproved of Rubens. His brief notes of the works have survived, and demonstrate his close attention to detail. Of Titian's *The Entombment*, he writes that 'Mary is in blue which partakes of crimson tone, and by it unites with the bluer sky'. The emphasis here, and in other of his notes, is upon the colours employed by the artist. His is almost a technical examination of pictorial effect; he is investigating the professional skills of other artists in order to learn from them.

The results of his travels were on display in the exhibition of 1803. He portrayed his turbulent arrival in France with a seascape, *Calais Pier*, that was accompanied by oil-paintings set in the regions of Bonneville and Mâcon. The latter, entitled *The Festival upon the Opening of the Vintage of Mâcon*, was executed in Claude's grandest manner; the setting, however, owes less to France than to the Thames by Richmond. The landscape itself is irradiated by a strong human presence, with labourers dancing or reclining; these figures reaffirm Turner's interest in work and activity. He had a strong preoccupation with labour, and with rest after labour. He had a deep interest in the prospect of endurance through time. But these are also figures bound in communion with a specific place, as if they had grown out of the earth and belonged to it. It was one of his visionary conceptions.

There is also an oil-painting of the *Holy Family*, inspired by seeing Titian in the Louvre, but it failed to find a purchaser. His critics accused him of painting 'blots' or 'embrios', of creating works in which the viewer had to imagine what was being shown, which suggests that they had already divined the indeterminacy and freedom of Turner's vision. His paintings were 'unfinished' and the subjects were not 'made out' in any formal sense.

His independence was underlined by his decision to open a gallery of his work in the spring of 1804 – just three days after the death of his mother in Bethlehem Hospital. It was not unusual for artists to have private galleries, but it was surprising for an artist not yet thirty to embark on the enterprise; it was another mark of his self-confidence. The gallery was situated on the first floor of his house in Harley Street, in an extension that covered part of the garden, and became in essence a private showroom where selected guests could wander and wonder. It was not particularly large – a plan of the site shows an 'outbuilding' some sixteen feet by thirty-eight feet – but it became the home for the majority of his paintings and the primary source of his income. He referred to it as 'the shop'. Indeed some of his oil-paintings were now being sold to private dealers for three or four hundred guineas.

He seems also to have been particular about less important financial matters; he used to charge his patrons and buyers for the frames. But prospective purchasers were not discouraged. He sold his work to collectors of 'Old Masters', such as Beckford himself, and also to successful fellow artists. He had no 'agent' until a much later date in his career, but he was not deficient in the arts of the salesman. In any case, as one artist put it at the time, why should he not ask such prices when no one else could paint such pictures?

But the gallery was more than just a commercial enterprise. He thought of his canvases as a 'family', and he often became permanently attached to certain favoured family members. He disliked selling them, and in some cases refused to do so, and was heard to enquire, 'What is the use of them but together?' In his will, he stipulated his purpose of 'keeping my works together'. It is an understandable impulse, perhaps, in an artist who had a keen sense of his historical achievement no less than of his visionary purpose. He wanted his audience to understand the complete statement.

No catalogue of the first exhibition in Harley Street has survived, although a painting on panel of *Old Margate Pier* is a likely candidate for inclusion there. But his business at home did not prevent him from exhibiting at the Royal Academy in the same year; in fact, to get away from the noise of the builders in Harley Street, he worked upon one canvas in the Keeper's rooms of that institution. It was entitled *Boats Carrying Out Anchors and Cables to Dutch Men of War in 1665*, and it was accompanied by *Narcissus and Echo*. He was exhibiting his range, albeit with the twin themes of water turbulent and water limpid. There was also a further extension of that range in a startlingly different direction. Appended to the entry of *Narcissus and Echo*, in the exhibition catalogue, there were some verses composed by Turner himself. He had already included lines by Milton to describe earlier paintings, as a way of setting the context for a painted scene, but this seems to have been the first occasion when he wrote his own. They became something of a custom, too, and purported to come from an unfinished epic poem entitled 'The Fallacies of Hope'. He never published any final or finished version of the poem, and it is entirely likely that it never existed except in his own mind. It existed, perhaps, only to provide quotations for his finished paintings.

Mezzotint of *The Shipwreck* (1805), the first of Turner's paintings to be engraved. This was an important step in Turner's career: prints were sold for £2.2s and proofs for £4.4s.

In his poetry the emblem of chaos and destruction is the shipwreck. And in the private gallery on Harley Street, in the following year, 1805, he showed what was perhaps his most famous painting to date. *The Shipwreck* – or *The Storm* as it was originally called – displayed to John Ruskin 'infinitely more power of figure painting than ever landscape painter showed before'. The great masses of water, the sweeping diagonals of sails and masts, the heaving vortex at the centre of the composition, impart to it a truly awe-ful authority. A later critic has suggested that in this work Turner 'had become possessed by the true genius of oil painting'. But of course he had also become possessed by the wild sea. Although we may be given some leave to doubt the actual truth of the anecdote of Turner strapped to the mast (p. 138), which he assiduously promoted, it does emphasise the evident fact that he seems almost to identify with the elements of storm and sea. As Titus says in Shakespeare's play, *Titus Andronicus*, 'I am the sea.'

The Shipwreck was the first of Turner's oil-paintings to be engraved, and thus became the first in a series of works that would help to enlarge the artist's reputation beyond the ranks of the collectors and the dealers. He would also begin to illustrate the works of poets and novelists for the purposes of engraving. In his dealings with printers he was thorough, succinct and practical; he bargained with them shrewdly, and oversaw their work with a careful eye. He was a good man of business, in other words, whose professionalism touched every aspect of his life.

Chapter Four
1805–1811

After the Battle of Trafalgar, in the autumn of 1805, the body of Nelson was brought by the *Victory* to the mouth of the Thames. Turner was given permission to board the boat and to make sketches, drawings, and notes of the occasion. He interviewed members of the crew and carefully wrote down the details of their appearance, all in preparation for the grand canvas he was about to begin. 'C. Hardy rather tall,' he jotted down, 'looks dreadful . . . fair, about 36 years.'

He saw the Thames in a less haunted and funereal mood when he rented a riverside house in the village of Isleworth, not far from Richmond – a place that, in his canvases, becomes enchanted. It was a medium-sized house, double-fronted, with a summer-house at the bottom of the garden beside the water. It was called Syon Ferry House, because the ferry itself shuttled between his front door (so to speak) and the deer park at Richmond. He started a new sketchbook which he entitled 'Studies for Pictures, Isleworth'. He drew scenes along the river-bank, and the boats which sailed along the river itself.

Yet he had another subject. In other sketchbooks of the period he introduced classical motifs and figures. In one book he noted down the titles of possible paintings, among them 'Dido and Aeneas', 'The Parting of Brutus and Portia',

The pavilion, near Isleworth where Turner lived in Syon Ferry House on the Thames during 1805 and '06. The design shows an idyllic scene worthy of Claude, the painter whom Turner most admired.

and 'Jason Arriving at Colchis'. He was extending his field of vision. He had been reading widely in classical literature with the help of the best translations, Pope's versions of Homer and Dryden's versions of Virgil among them. He also bought all thirteen volumes of an anthology entitled *The Works of the British Poets*, which suggests that he was embarking upon a serious and single-minded course of self-education; he was always very thorough, and determined, in his preparations. He had purchased casts of the marbles that

Lord Elgin had recently brought back from Greece, and in a letter to the noble peer or thief (according to taste) he congratulated him on rescuing work from 'the most brilliant period of human nature'. For him the classical world was a dream of nobility and beauty, a vast reservoir of profound feeling and repository of inspired thought.

Yet the Thames also inspired him. It was for him in part an allegorical river along which the figures of myth or legend might be depicted. In one sketchbook he quoted some lines of Pope which celebrate 'the silver Thames'. But if for him it aroused contemplations of classical antiquity, these were placed in the service of his art. It is clear enough, from his jottings and his musings, that he wished to elevate landscape painting into the highest regions of artistic endeavour. He wanted it to emulate the claims of historical painting, and become the medium of allegorical and moral truth. He was intent on being – in the conventional sense, perhaps – a 'great' painter. But he would do it on his own terms.

So what did he do next? He built himself a boat. He noted down the cost of sails and rigging, mast and pump. He was going to be part of the river's life, to draw and paint while being carried along its waters, and to enjoy the benefits of close observation. He had known the Thames since his earliest years, and had sailed upon it many times; to own a boat must have been a dream of his childhood. He sailed upstream to Hampton Court and Windsor, and then onwards to Reading and Oxford; then he went down to the Port of London and the estuary. He completed an extraordinary number of sketches and drawings, as if the fluency of the river itself had inspired him. There are

miraculous studies of the trees bending across the river-
bank, of barges unloading, of the shadows of buildings on
the water. Many of his later oil-paintings are based upon
these brief studies.

But he also completed some oil-paintings directly on to
wooden board or canvas, experimenting with the possibilities of light and tone *en plein air*. He had a portable
paint-box (which still survives) with his various pigments
wrapped up in bladders. His vision was so powerful and
immediate that it could only be captured on the spot. In his
water-colour sketches, too, he quickly daubed on the
colours and tones with the freedom and spontaneity of fresh
inspiration. There were occasions when he drove the paint
with his fingers; the colours change as they intermingle.

When later in the year he sailed downstream to the Pool
of London, the riverine landscape of the 'silver Thames' was
displaced by the black mud and dirt of the working river. He
knew this aspect of the river well, as the site of human energy
and activity; it was here that he sketched ketches and cutters
and guard ships. There is even the calculation of the size of
a canvas sail, jotted down on the side of one drawing.

He was in the process preparing himself for the work that
he had contemplated ever since visiting the *Victory* anchored
off Sheerness the year before. This was *The Battle of
Trafalgar, as seen from the Mizen Starboard Shrouds of the
Victory*. It was exhibited at his gallery in Harley Street, and
met with a mixed response. Farington described it as 'very
crude' and 'unfinished'; Turner seems in part to have agreed
with the criticism because he reworked the painting, and
exhibited it again two years later. On the second occasion
the artist, John Landseer, considered it to be a 'British epic

picture' and 'the first picture of the kind that has ever, to our knowledge, been exhibited'.

The other painting that he exhibited in this year, 1806, was of disharmony in a different key. It was entitled *The Goddess of Discord choosing the Apple of Contention in the Garden of Hesperides* – even the length of the title suggests the seriousness of Turner's intent – and it was shown at the British Institution, a new organisation established in three rooms in Pall Mall to enhance the reputation of British art. For its first exhibition he had chosen once more to depict a classical subject as a statement of his ambition.

He also sent a painting to the Royal Academy, of course, but was incensed when it was badly hung in the exhibition room. These were matters of intense importance to the Academicians, and to the public, who were rightly annoyed when work was not seen to its best advantage. The painting itself was entitled *Fall of the Rhine at Schaffhausen*, and is a fine expression of the movement of powerful waters between rocks. At the time, however, it provoked severe criticism for its extravagance. The comments of two newspaper editors, present at the opening, have been recorded. 'That is Madness,' one observed on looking at Turner's canvas. The other concurred with 'He is a madman.' The charge of madness was often brought against him in subsequent years and, although it is one he generally ignored, the history of his mother's lunacy cannot fail to have rendered him sensitive to the subject.

A visit to a fellow artist in Kent this year provides an opportunity to see Turner in a more entertaining light. The daughter of his close friend, W.F. Wells, recalls the young artist as 'light-hearted' and 'merry', filled with 'laughter and fun' particularly in the company of children. On one occasion he was sitting on the ground 'with the children winding his ridiculously large cravat round his neck'. He exclaimed to her, 'See here, Clara, what these children are about!' And she also recalls the occasion of his climbing up a tree, to paint from a different vantage, and of her passing the colours up to him. She adds, interestingly enough, that 'his feelings were seldom seen on the surface, but they were deep and enduring. No one would have imagined, under that rather rough and cold exterior, how very strong were the affections which lay hidden beneath.' It is testimony to the essential humanity of the man.

This happy trip also produced some unexpected results. W.F. Wells conceived the idea that Turner should embark upon a series of landscape drawings, of all kinds and in all settings, that would then be engraved under Turner's own direct supervision. 'For your own credit's sake,' his daughter remembered him telling the artist, 'you ought to give a work to the public which will do you justice.' He was referring here not to the manifest superiority of Turner's painting, but to the possibility of engraving work that might after his death be shoddily executed. Turner should provide a living example. Turner is supposed to have replied that 'there will be no peace with you till I begin. Well, give me a sheet of paper there, rule the size for me, tell me what subject I shall take.' He completed the first five drawings, with pen and brush, in the company of Wells and his family in Kent; they were then dispatched to the engraver, Charles Turner. He had previously executed the engraving of *The Shipwreck*, and was deemed to be ingenious and trustworthy.

And so commenced a sequence of works which were given the general title of *Liber Studiorum*. His title was inspired by Claude's *Liber Veritatis* – Claude being the artist he most wanted to emulate. His intention was to publish two parts every year, each part containing five prints with a frontispiece. His purpose was to create a *magnum opus* that might rival the work of Claude, and he divided his productions into six different categories – Historical, Pastoral, Elevated Pastoral, Mountain, Marine and Architectural. It was conceived as a complete statement, and once more suggests Turner's desire to move on and conquer each new territory. He was an over-reacher as well as an over-turner.

It was a series that could have gone on until his death, but in fact he managed only some fourteen parts, and seventy-one engravings, altogether. He was sole publisher, using various engravers as his technicians – although he did engrave for himself eight of his drawings. As might have been expected, he was an exacting employer who relied upon the strictest standards of line and tone. He executed the drawings in sepia ink with water-colour, marking out the salient features in pen and washing in the shading with brush; from these original drawings the engraver would then work, cutting the lines into the soft wax of the copper plate. One engraver recalled how Turner would often go to Hampstead, and 'would spend hours on the heath studying the effects of atmosphere and the changes of light and shade, and the gradations required to express them'. Engraving is in certain respects the art of light and shade. It was natural and fitting that Turner, of all painters, should be drawn towards it.

*

By the beginning of 1807 he had moved down-river from Isleworth to Hammersmith, where his address was 6 West End, Upper Mall. The house has been described as modest and comfortable but, more importantly, its garden ran down to the bank; Turner seems not to have been able to live away from water for very long. The Thames was the centre of his being. In the garden there was also a summer-house, which he used as a studio. Here he laid his water-colours on the floor to dry. When a friend expressed some surprise that he could work in such humble surroundings he replied that 'lights and a room were absurdities and that a picture could be painted anywhere'. It was part of his sturdy practicality in all matters pertaining to his art.

The neighbourhood itself proved to be less than ideal, however, since the area behind his house was soon being dug up for the creation by the Middlesex Water Company of the West Middlesex Water Works. This did not prevent Turner from speculating in land in other locations. He bought at auction for ninety-five pounds a cottage and half an acre of ground near Great Missenden in Buckinghamshire; this may have been designed to harbour Sarah Danby and her children. In the spring of 1807 he also purchased some land in Twickenham. Here he began making plans for the construction of a villa, a gentleman's residence appropriate to his situation in life. There is no reason why an artist of genius should not also be an astute businessman.

In this period he lived with his father in Hammersmith, and commuted to his gallery in Harley Street – a journey of some two hours by foot, which was no great distance for either father or son. He was in fact more than ever engaged in London life. He was busily involved in the publication of his *Liber Studiorum*, for example, the first number of which was published in the summer of this year. It included five separate plates, engraved by Charles Turner from Turner's recent drawings of the Thames. Turner the artist, however, was something of a martinet with Turner the engraver. In the following year he left a peremptory note upon a proof, stating: 'Sir, You have done in aquatint all the Castle down to the rocks: Did I ever ask for such an indulgence?'

He was exhibiting at his own gallery, of course, and in this year he displayed *Sheerness and the Isle of Sheppey, with the Junction of the Thames and the Medway from the Nore* together with other Thames views. In most of these paintings the river itself is shown at peace, with all the signs of human labour decorating its banks, but *Sheerness and the Isle of Sheppey* depicts more turbulent and dangerous waters. These are the twin poles of Turner's imagination, serenity and storm, tranquillity and chaos.

He was also exhibiting at the Royal Academy works of a quite different character. One oil-painting is entitled *A Country Blacksmith disputing upon the Price of Iron, and the Price charged to the Butcher for shoeing his Poney*. This homely if prosaic title is in itself an indication that Turner was trying his hand at the anecdotal or realistic genre of painting inaugurated by the Flemish painter Teniers the Younger, but recently made fashionable by the Scottish artist David Wilkie. The year before, Wilkie's *Village Politicians* had been judged the success of the show; Turner was not to be outdone, especially by an artist some ten years younger, and so he set out to prove that he could manage the same kind of painting with more skill and fluency.

He also exhibited *Sun Rising Through Vapour; Fishermen cleaning and selling Fish*, in a literal manner outshining Wilkie's *The Blind Fiddler* of the same year. The conflation of 'sun' and 'vapour' already suggests Turner's later sense of palpable light and incandescence. It was reported that Turner had deliberately reddened his sun so that it would cast into shade Wilkie's contribution. This is in fact inaccurate, since the solar disc is mysterious and pale, but it is clear that Turner did not necessarily welcome competitors. When one collector asked him the price of the *Blacksmith* painting he replied 'that he understood Wilkie was to have 100 guineas for his *Blind Fiddler* and he should not rate his picture at a less price'. He was always of a combative nature. His connection with the Royal Academy was strengthened this year, when he was appointed Professor of Perspective. He was in fact the only candidate for the position, and so his election was assured. But he delayed four years before giving his first lecture.

While his father was busy in the house and garden at Hammersmith, Turner acquired a new caretaker for his gallery in Harley Street. Hannah Danby was the niece of his mistress, Sarah Danby, and at the age of twenty-three became a permanent presence in Turner's life. She remained his caretaker and general custodian until his death, becoming increasingly more eccentric as the years passed; but she was loyal and reliable. It has been rumoured that their relationship was more than that of employer and servant, and that it was she who bore his children, but this seems to have been a case of mistaken identity between the two women who both had the name Danby. Sarah Danby, however, seems to play a less important role in the artist's life from this time forward.

He was moving in 'society' now more than ever – or, rather, he was visiting the country houses of prospective patrons with a view to painting their estates. In 1808 he spent some weeks at Tabley House in Cheshire, for example, and completed two views of that stately home for its owner Sir John Leicester. The finished paintings were exhibited at the Royal Academy in the following year, when one newspaper critic said that 'mere topography' had in the case of Turner been transformed by a 'magic pencil'. Magic is not cheap. It was estimated that the paintings were 'of Turner's 250 guineas size'.

Turner was not always at work, however, while on the estates of his patrons. Another guest at the house recalled that he 'was occupied in *fishing* rather than painting'. He was indeed a keen and proficient angler, and in that characteristic state of suspended animation he dreamed of verse and painting. He observed, too, the multitudinous effects of the sun upon the water. He often had with him on his travels a copy of Izaak Walton's *The Compleat Angler*, and apparently owned an umbrella which by some strange act of transmogrification became a fishing rod. When he got a bite, according to one observer, 'he appeared as much pleased as a boy at school'. A friend, accompanying him on another expedition, has left a description of his behaviour. 'Every fish he caught he showed to me, and appealed to me to decide whether the size justified him to keep it for the table, or to return it to the river. His hesitation was often almost touching, and he always gave the prisoner at the bar the benefit of the doubt.' It was not for him simply a pastime. He completed many paintings of fishermen, at work on the sea or on the sands, and included anglers within his landscapes; he even sketched 'still lives' of four fish or what he called in one of his verses 'the finny race'.

He also visited Petworth House, the home of Lord Egremont, in this year. There is an account of a later journey to that house where Turner was seen, by a boy, 'smoking a cigar, and on the grass, near him, lay a fine pike'. But the artist's tackle became entwined with some roots, and a boat was despatched to help clear the tangle of line. 'While waiting for the boat,' the boy recalled, 'Turner became quite chatty, rigging me a little ship, cut out of a chip, sticking

Young Anglers. Turner loved fishing and enjoyed romping with children. He etched this himself. The scene is Marylebone Fields, not far from his studio in Queen Anne Street.

masts into it, and making her sails from a leaf or two torn from a small sketch book, in which I recollect seeing a memorandum in colour that he had made of the sea and sunset.' He was always good with children, and seemed effortlessly able to enter their world. The account ends with a picture of Turner walking back to Petworth House, holding the pike in one hand, with a bundle of sketches in the pocket of his coat.

He stayed at Petworth many times after his first visit in 1808, and it became the site and context for many of his most celebrated paintings. Here he came under the amiable patronage of Lord Egremont, who had first purchased a work from him in 1802. Egremont was more relaxed and casual than most of his peers, a man of few words, a welcoming host to painters and writers, and decidedly unconventional in his behaviour. Lord Blessington observed that

> nothing will convince Lady Spenser that Lord Egremont has not forty-three Children, who all live in the House with him and their respective Mothers; and that the latter are usually kept in the background but when quarrels arise, which few days pass without, each mother takes part with her Progeny, bursts into the drawing room, fights with each other, Lord E, his children, and, I believe, the Company, and makes scenes worthy of a Billingsgate or a Madhouse.

Egremont was immensely wealthy, of course, but sensitive to Turner's peculiar genius. It is likely that Turner, himself considered odd or unusual, responded warmly to what were

called Egremont's 'eccentric habits'. It was said by one guest
at Petworth that the host's

> peculiarities . . . were utterly incompatible with
> conversation, or any prolonged discussion. He
> never remained five minutes in the same place, and
> was continually oscillating between the library and
> his bedroom, or wandering about the enormous
> house in all directions; sometimes he broke off in
> the middle of a conversation on some subject which
> appeared to interest him, and disappeared, and an
> hour after, on casual meeting, would resume just
> where he left off.

Such foibles would not have disturbed Turner in the least.
Egremont seems in fact to have given the painter an open
invitation to stay that, in later years, was willingly accepted.
He did not commission paintings from Turner, but allowed
the artist to use his house and his estate as a living studio.
Some of the artist's most famous works – *Petworth: The Old
Library* and *The Apotheosis of Lord Egremont (Interior at
Petworth)* among them – are the result of his enlightened
patronage. Turner also completed a series of Petworth
drawings on blue paper which evoke specific scenes and
objects.

Petworth was a large and elaborate house, with a
succession of rooms on the ground floor that lent it the
aspect of a Renaissance palace; the White Library, the
Marble Hall, the Carved Room, the Square Dining-Room,
the Red Room and the North Gallery were all exquisitely
furnished and decorated. One visitor recollected that

Every door of every room was wide open from one
end to the other, and from the front to behind,
whichever way you looked; and not a human being
visible . . . but the magnitude of the space being
seen all at once – the scale of every room, gallery,
passage etcetera, the infinity of pictures and statues
throughout, made as agreeable an impression on
me as I ever witnessed.

Turner and Egremont often discussed painting together,
and one butler remembered an argument between them
concerning some vegetables that Turner had depicted
floating on the water in *Brighton from the Sea*. The amiable
earl insisted that they would have sunk, whereas the painter
was equally adamant that they would float as he had painted
them. A tub of water and some identical vegetables were
then called for; when they were placed in the water, they did
indeed sink. But Turner never altered his painting. He
remained true to his visionary conception. He was also very
stubborn.

But by 1808 Turner had made the acquaintance of another
rich and enlightened patron. Walter Fawkes had been a
member of parliament for Yorkshire, with firm opinions on
the importance of democratic change. Like Egremont, he
was a progressive landowner and estate manager. Turner
visited him at his country house in Yorkshire, Farnley Hall,
over a period of sixteen years, characteristically in the
summer or autumn. It was a medley of a house, part
Jacobean and part late eighteenth-century (the contemporary sections having been commissioned by Fawkes

The East Lodge gates, made to Turner's own design, at Farnley Hall, home of Walter Fawkes. Turner's complete set of drawings of his patron's house, set in its park overlooking the Wharfe valley, were known affectionately as his 'Wharfedales'. Turner mourned the death of Fawkes in 1825 ('my good Auld lang sine is gone') and never again returned to Farnley Hall.

himself); it also contained a private museum of Civil War artefacts and memorabilia, some of which the artist drew. Turner was given his own suite of rooms, including a studio, where he was invited to stay even when the Fawkeses were not in residence. Fawkes also became an important and munificent patron of the artist, commissioning both oils and water-colours. The daughters of the house soon became accustomed to this unusual guest, and have left recollections of Turner both at work and at play. They recalled him engaged upon his water-colours, 'cords spread across the room as in that of a washerwoman, and papers tinted with pink, and blue, and yellow, hanging on them to dry'.

The oldest son of the house, Hawksworth, had other memories. He recalled the artist rapt in the contemplation of a thunderstorm, making notes of its form and colour on a scrap of paper. 'Isn't it grand?' Turner asked the young man. 'Isn't it wonderful? Isn't it sublime?' Hawksworth recalled how

> he was absorbed – he was entranced. There was the storm rolling and sweeping and shafting out its lightning over the Yorkshire hills. Presently the storm passed, and he finished. 'There, Hawkey,' he said. 'In two years time you will see this again, and call it Hannibal crossing the Alps.'

The allusion is almost too good, and too precise, to be true. Nevertheless the image of Turner, watching the uproar in the heavens and imagining it above the heads of Hannibal and his troops, is an evocative one.

There is perhaps more substance to another account of Turner at Farnley Hall. Walter Fawkes had asked the artist to draw a man-of-war, and Turner rose to the challenge. It seems that he began by pouring wet paint till it [the paper] was saturated, he tore, he scratched, he scrubbed at it in a kind of frenzy and the whole thing was chaos – but gradually and as if by magic the lovely ship, with all its exquisite minutiae, came into being and by luncheon time the drawing was taken down in triumph.

This emergence of form out of chaos, the man-of-war emerging mysteriously from a mist of colour, is an apt description of Turner's painterly method. He created a dynamic and fluid space in which to work, quite unlike the more rigidly defined ground of previous artists. His tactile sense of creating shape and form – scratching and scrubbing as if he were dealing with some recalcitrant material – gives his work the texture of inspired improvisation and magical creation.

These forays into country-house society did not, however, prevent him from fulfilling his usual roll-call of exhibitions. He re-exhibited *The Battle of Trafalgar* at the British Institution, after its relative failure two years previously in his own gallery. At the Harley Street gallery itself, in 1808, he exhibited a plethora of paintings depicting the Thames. It had become his great subject. Many of them were praised for their 'Claude-like serenity', particularly *Pope's Villa at Twickenham* and *View of Richmond Hill and Bridge*, in which the glowing light lends breadth and spaciousness to the scenes. There are other paintings of the sea, such as *Margate* and *Sheerness from the Nore*, in which Turner demonstrates his mastery of the delineation of bodies of water – transparent or shadowed, rising or falling, always in vibrant movement.

He chose quite another kind of painting for the Royal Academy show in 1808, exhibiting a single work entitled *The Unpaid Bill, or the Dentist Reproving His Son's Prodigality;* as its title suggests, it was an anecdotal picture in which father expostulates with son. There are some papers on the floor, with the phrase 'Tooth drawn' clearly visible. It is hard not to feel, however, that Turner's real attention was lavished upon all the tools of the dentist's trade. One half of the painting, caught in the rays of the sun, shows basins and phials, glasses and crucibles, laid out in profusion. There is also a parrot, although this may be Turner's surreptitious sign for himself. His features, in profile, were often compared to that talkative bird's. (See p. 1.)

In the following year he was once more exhibiting at Harley Street and the Royal Academy. No less than thirteen canvases were hung in his own gallery, manifesting the range and variety of his artistic concerns. There were riverscape and seascape; there was the classical grandeur of *Thomson's Aeolian Harp* as well as the painterly realism of *Harvest Dinner, Kingston Bank*. The unforced tenderness and simplicity of this latter painting, with the labourers pausing to rest, to wash, and to eat, manifest all the sympathy of Turner's nature in relation to the poor and the humble of the world. To one of these paintings in the Harley Street gallery he appended his signature with the initials 'PP'. This is to be deciphered as Professor of Perspective.

A painting expedition to Oxford in the early months of 1810 suggests his practical, rather than theoretical, approach to his subject. He had been asked by a publisher to complete a view of the High Street in that city as a preliminary to a large engraving. He was happy to accept the commission, and set out his terms in a very businesslike manner – 'my Pictures are all 3 Feet by 4 Feet, 200 gs [guineas], half which size will be 100, but should not mind an inch or two'. On the agreement of terms he travelled up to Oxford and made a pencil sketch of the street from a hackney coach. But he was very concerned about details. He wished to know how the windows in the High Street were glazed, and whether they projected in a bow. He was also about to introduce some academic figures and wished to know 'what kind of staff the Beadles use, and if they wear caps?' No junior draughtsman could have been more exact or particular. When the painting was complete, he was unhappy about the height of the spire of St Mary's Church. He informed the publisher that 'it shall be altered to measure'. Despite the fact that he was 'so very busy', as he put it in a letter, the work was finished to the deadline already proposed. He was in every sense a professional workman who prided himself on his expedition and punctuality. The publisher was so pleased with the result that he sent Turner a present of sausages.

He was, as we have seen, also a good economist. In this year he was intent on purchasing land as an investment; he bought some acres at Richmond for four hundred pounds, and some land at Lee Common in Buckinghamshire for £102. He also bought shares in the Atlas Fire Office; he might profit from fiery spectacles in more than an artistic sense. His finances are open for inspection by posterity. He jotted down notes on his savings and holdings on odd pages of his sketchbooks; we know, for example, that by the summer of 1810 he had more than twenty thousand pounds in 'Reduced 3% Annuities' and more than four thousand pounds in 'Navy 5%'. He also kept lists of the sales of his paintings, with the names of the purchasers in the right-hand column. He was methodical. He bought property, too. One acquaintance noted that 'He would occasionally look in at the auction mart by the Bank; and on one of these occasions it occurred to him that two houses were about to be knocked down at a very low figure; he bid, and got them.' With property came the eternal problem of tenants, some of whom proved refractory. He was not always severe with them, however. At his death it was discovered that for some years he had not claimed rent from one recalcitrant tenant.

In the Royal Academy this year he exhibited three paintings devoted to the stately homes of his patrons, two of Lowther Castle in Westmorland, the home of the earl of Lonsdale, and one entitled *Petworth, Sussex, the Seat of the Earl of Egremont: Dewy Morning*. He hoped to evoke the freshness and lightness of the morning dew with what was for him still a novel technique in oils. He covered the canvas with a white ground, thus lending a bright and pellucid quality to the paint applied to it. It was an effect he had attained in water-colours, by employing white drawing-paper which, as it were, shone through the washes of colour, and in *Petworth . . . Dewy Morning* the expanses of water and of sky have a wonderful radiance.

He returned to some of his favourite subjects in the Harley Street exhibition of this year – a lake, a bridge, an ancient palace, a ruined castle, an avalanche, and a fishmarket on a beach. A surreal and synoptic painting by Turner would have to contain all of these elements. There is a story concerning the painting of the fishmarket that added to the legend of the artist's parsimony. He brought *Fishmarket on the Sands* to its purchaser by coach, received a cheque for its safe delivery and left; but he returned two or three minutes later, and asked for three shillings to cover the cab-fare.

In the following year there was no exhibition in Harley Street. He had decided to alter the gallery and to provide it with a new entrance, around the corner in Queen Anne Street, but as a result he found himself 'surrounded by rubbish and paint'. But he continued his work, and to the Royal Academy this year he delivered two great classical subjects, *Apollo and Python* and *Mercury and Hersoé*. The latter was inspired by Veronese, but owes its manner to Claude. Its coolness and limpidity, its subtle gradation of tone and colours, its harmonious composition, suggest Turner's painterly allegiances. It was praised very highly at the time and when the Prince Regent spoke at the Academy banquet he alluded to 'landscapes which Claude would have admired'. The newspapers described it as a 'master-piece' and 'very fine'. *The Sun* in particular was very enthusiastic and said that the artist 'had exceeded all that we or his most partial admirers could expect from his powers'. Turner was so pleased with this notice that he copied it out in his notebook, and wrote a letter of thanks to the editor. This suggests that, despite his own disparagement of newspaper reviewers, he was not entirely immune to criticism. His attitude of indifference was really only a shield against disappointment and hurt.

Chapter Five
1811

Turner returned to the Royal Academy in another capacity in January 1811, since it was in this year that he gave his first lectures as Professor of Perspective. He had been appointed to this post four years before, but nervousness or dilatoriness had kept him away from the lectern. He was worried about his delivery, and jotted down notes in advance on oratorical style and pronunciation. He was in fact never a very conscientious professor; he held the post for thirty years, but managed to give only twelve sets of lectures. On this first occasion there were six lectures, delivered on successive Monday evenings, with such themes as 'angular perspective' and 'aerial perspective'. He was concerned with the properties of shadows and the nature of reflection. There is a surviving diagram, of glass balls partly filled with water, which he used to complement his words.

In the last lecture, however, he seems to have forsaken this somewhat dry or demanding discipline for an account of landscape painting and architectural setting. He concluded the series with a paean to national pride when he told those assembled that the nation must look to them 'for the further advancement of the profession . . . looking forward with the hope that ultimately the joint endeavours of concording abilities will in the pursuit of all that is meritorious

Reflections and refractions in two transparent globes, one half-filled with water. Turner was demonstrating the effect of light on curved surfaces.

irrevocably fix the united Standard of Arts in the British Empire'. His polysyllables are quite a mouthful, but his patriotic message is clear enough.

Perspective was in some respects a difficult and technically challenging subject, problems compounded by the fact that Turner was not himself a particularly good lecturer. His delivery was not entirely clear, but his manner was compensated by the drawings which he presented as illustrations to his thesis. One of those who attended the lectures recalled that

> half of each lecture was addressed to the attendant behind him, who was constantly busied, under his muttered directions, in selecting from a huge portfolio of drawings and diagrams to illustrate his

teaching; many of these were truly beautiful, speaking intelligibly enough to the eye, if his language did not to the ear.

The librarian of the Royal Academy was a constant attendant of these occasions and remarked that 'there is much to *see* at Turner's lectures – much that I delight in seeing, though I cannot hear him'.

The artist William Frith has left a description of Turner speaking on another occasion with 'the stammering, the long pauses, the bewildering mystery of it, required to be witnessed for any adequate idea to be formed'. And then he recorded Turner's actual words – '"Gentlemen, I see some –" (pause and another look round) "new faces at this – table – Well – do you – do any of you – I mean – Roman History" (a pause). "There is no doubt, at least I hope not, that you are acquainted – no, unacquainted – that is to say – of course, why not? . . ."'

He had a deep voice and a recognisably Cockney accent, sometimes dropping his 'h's in the approved London style. One periodical writer adverted to his 'vulgarity of pronunciation', referring to mathematics as 'mithematics', having as 'haiving', and foolery as 'follery'. Ruskin reports a conversation of Turner's, in which he uttered the phrase 'Ain't they worth more?' This is hardly in the class of Dickens's Sam Weller, and is essentially standard London diction, but it provoked patronising comments. For those who did not possess genius themselves, it was enough that Turner was not a 'gentleman'.

The point is, of course, that like William Blake and William Hogarth – two artists whom in attitude and

demeanour he so much resembled – he was a quin-
tessentially London genius, a Cockney visionary. He could
never leave for long what he called 'the loadstone London',
loadstone here meaning a magnet. He loved crowds, and
smoke and glare, and soot and dust and dunghills. The
occasional theatricality of his art also betrays his London
inheritance. In his work he was perhaps not interested in
particular persons – many of the individuals in his canvases
were said to resemble the creatures of that popular urban
art, Punch and Judy – but in the broad general movement
of light and colour.

His contemporaries often criticised the 'crude' theatricality of his paintings, but they were really only recognising his
love of transcendent spectacle. It has already been observed
how he began his career as a scene-painter at the Pantheon,
and like many other London artists he had an affection for
the grand effects which were possible in that medium. One
contemporary, on seeing *Dido building Carthage, or the
Rise of the Carthaginian Empire*, remarked that he felt as if
he were in the presence of the most splendid 'drop-scenes'
in a theatre. Turner often chose to paint fires and
shipwrecks, when these subjects were the stock in trade of
nineteenth-century ballets and melodramas. He loved fire in
all of its moods and conditions. He resembles the fire-
watcher in *The Old Curiosity Shop*, who sits before the
furnace of a factory and whispers, 'It's my memory, that fire,
and shows me all my life.'

Indeed it has been stated that Turner's paintings did
themselves change the art of scenery in the Victorian period.
'Scenery now becomes a source of attraction . . .' a critic
wrote in 1848. 'Now this change we owe to Turner.' There

is no reason at all why the artist would have forsworn this legacy. He himself once declared that his inspiration for his famous painting *Ulysses deriding Polyphemus* came not from Homer but from a song in a pantomime entitled *Melodrame Mad*:

> I sing the cave of Polypheme,
> Ulysses made him cry out,
> For he ate his mutton, drank his wine,
> And then he poked his eye out.

Turner may have been ironic, but his instinctive reaching for the songs of the popular stage does suggest his own affinities.

Like other Londoners, too, he was by instinct a dissenter and nonconformist. He was touched by the general egalitarianism of the citizenry; although many of his patrons were noblemen, he retained a sturdy independence of spirit and of conduct. He moved among printers and engravers, who were well known in London for their radical turn of mind. He had an especial fondness for John Wycliffe and George Fox, who in the fourteenth century and seventeenth century respectively challenged the orthodox rituals of the established faith. In later life he seems implicitly to have supported the causes of Greek independence and Hungarian independence. His close friend Walter Fawkes, who was an MP, was intent upon maintaining 'the people's defence against aristocratic domination and royal despotism'. So we may safely conclude that Turner himself was a reformer.

Yet, more significantly, he had a symbolic vision of the world, a world filled for him with mythic correspondences and spiritual associations. He was preoccupied with emblem and with allegory, in a culture becoming increasingly dominated by fact and statistic. He was in the conventional sense of his period a thoroughly irreligious man, and paid no attention to the rituals and observances of the Established Church, but his faith was of quite a different kind. There is the apocryphal story of his muttering, on his death-bed, 'The sun is God.' If it is indeed a legend it is nevertheless an appropriate and convincing one. He understood the sacredness of light as the power which coursed through all things, and which charged the world with a divine grandeur. He had an almost primeval view of the heavens which, in sunlight or in moonlight, brooded over the earth. He bowed down to the deities of the cosmic order.

He is a Londoner, too, in his writings, In his familiar letters he displays a rambling urban vivacity, a tendency to veer off the point and to muddle his syntax. He had a brilliantly eclectic mind, picking up words and images while at the same time forging them in new and unexpected combinations. He conceived several ideas all at once, and sometimes forgot to separate them into their component parts. This was true of his lectures, too, in which brilliant perceptions were scattered in a wilderness of words. As he wrote on another occasion, 'The lake babbled not less, and the wind murmured not, nor the little fishes leaped for joy that their tormentor was not.'

This strangely contorted and convoluted style also characterises his verses, most of which were appended as commentaries upon his paintings. Like Blake, whose prophetic books bring words and images in exalted com-bination, Turner wished to make a complete statement. Like Blake, he seemed to consider the poet's role as being in part prophetic. His was a voice calling in the wilderness and, perhaps secretly, he had an elevated sense of his status and his vocation. And like Blake, too, he was often considered to be mad. He lacked, however, the poetic genius of Blake – compensated perhaps by the fact that by general agreement he is the greater artist.

He began composing verse in 1793, and never really stopped. He seemed to have composed at high speed, and in a variety of locations. He wrote verse all the time, jotting it down in the margins of books and on scraps of paper; he also had a particular notebook which he reserved for his poetry. That poetry, as it appears as an adjunct to his painting, is rich and cluttered. His surviving verses have a certain rough magic, and demonstrate his range. His poetry is perhaps too cerebral, however, employing as its model eighteenth-century versions of didactic and pastoral verse.

He had a particular love for James Thomson's *The Seasons*, an epic of natural observation that has not survived what Turner might have called the scythe of time. But it is interesting, in any event, that his principal literary model was from the genre of eighteenth century landscape poetry. His painting looked ahead, and his poetry looked behind. Yet the artist's verse is not wholly devoid of merit –

> surcharged
> With wrathful vapour, from the secret beds
> Where sleep the mineral generations drawn.
> Thence nitre, sulphur, and the fiery spume
> Of fat bitumen, streaming on the day,
> With barbarous-tinctured trains of latent flame,
> Pollute the sky.

He loved to represent conflict and cataclysm, chaos and confusion. The epic poem which he hoped to complete, 'The Fallacies of Hope', also suggests something of the interior imagination of Turner; its title suggests isolation and an anxiety not untouched by despair. There is a great difference, however, between his poetry and his painting. He thought when he wrote; he did not need to think when he painted or, rather, he employed a different kind of thinking which was much closer to the breath of his being. Some critics were ungenerous about his literary talent, but one friend looked at it in a more kindly light. 'Turner's thoughts', he said, 'were deeper than ordinary men can penetrate and much deeper than he could at any time describe.' Just as there was a deep mystery about his painting, so a lesser mystery – which we might call confusion – hovers about his words.

Chapter Six
1811–1813

He was busily engaged, in 1811, with selling copies of his *Liber Studiorum* from his own house. He had quarrelled with his engraver, Charles Turner, and in typically robust fashion had decided to publish them himself. But then in the summer he decided to extend his range of activity, as it were, by travelling to the West Country with a view to producing water-colours for engraving in a book entitled *Picturesque Views of the Southern Coast of England*. He needed to be perpetually busy, as if there were some great relief or release in continual activity. He prepared himself for the journey in his usual methodical fashion, going so far as to list the numbers and dates of the banknotes he was carrying with him. He listed all the places that he visited, too, among them the most picturesque spots in Dorset, Devon, Cornwall and Somerset. There were journeys to Corfe Castle and to Lulworth, to Lyme Regis and Land's End, Tintagel and Clovelly.

When in the neighbourhood of Barnstaple he took the opportunity of meeting his father's family. He and the West Country Turners may have stared at one another, without having much in particular to say. But he did feel some deep connection with his relatives. He returned to Devon on several occasions, and once told a friend: 'I am a Devon man – Barnstaple.' He was not of course a native of that place, and his remark could have been a piece of cheerful mis-representation. But the ties of family run very deep. When in Devon, perhaps the most echoic of English counties, he may have heard ancestral voices and felt a sense of belonging. He was away for some two months altogether, in which period he completed some two hundred pencil sketches.

He spent so much time in the West Country because he had become thoroughly disenchanted with his Hammer-smith home. The Middlesex Water Company had erected a 120-foot chimney behind his house, and the noise of construction and general labouring activity must have been immense. He was entranced by the industrial life of the river, but he did not appreciate it when it was literally at his back-door. So even now he was planning the construction of a house in a much quieter spot, further upstream in Twickenham. He had perhaps anticipated his move to the neighbourhood in a painting exhibited in 1808, *Pope's Villa at Twickenham*, in which he implicitly mourns the demolition of that hallowed spot in the previous year. So for him Twickenham was a place of sacred association.

He had purchased the land some four years before, but was now actively planning and sketching the design of his new villa. His youthful period as an architectural draughts-man proved its usefulness, and he finished many plans and elevations; he drew the rooms, and such details as the cornicing and the mantelpieces. He said that he had always wanted to be an architect, and now he had his opportunity. He even made himself responsible for the hiring of the builders and the labourers, and noted down the costs of landscaping the grounds – '100 Planting. 20 garden. 40 Pond.'

In this period, too, he fell ill. He seems to have been suffering from something he called 'Maltese Plague', the symptoms of which included 'Sickness, debility, shivering, heat, thirst, headache. Delirium, darkspots, ulcer.' It is not clear what combination of these distressing effects he suffered, but he smoked a narcotic herb to curb the effects of breathlessness. He may have believed himself to be growing old.

The house was erected in the course of 1812; it was a modest villa-like construction of two storeys, with a basement for a small scullery and kitchen. At the centre of the house, between the dining-room and the library, was Turner's studio filled with light. A serpentine staircase led to the two bedrooms on the first floor. There was a lily pond in the garden, and Turner planted a line of willow trees upon which he often gazed. Turner also ornamented the interior

Sandycombe Lodge. This small villa was designed and decorated by Turner himself, and built on land he had purchased at Twickenham.

of the house with models of ships in glass-cases, against which he painted the background of the sea. It was, in many respects, a perfect retreat.

At first Turner called it Solus Lodge, perhaps as testimony to the fact that he had finally parted from Sarah Danby. But the name was unwelcoming, and it was changed to Sandy-combe Lodge. In any case Turner did entertain guests. Fellow artists and fellow Academicians paid visits, to be regaled with cheese and porter or cake and wine. It has been described as a doll's house, neat and unpretending, but its neatness and simplicity testify also to the essential simplicity of Turner's nature. One young visitor remembered his visits to Twickenham where

> everything was of the most modest pretensions . . .
> The table cloth barely covered the table, and the
> earthenware was in strict keeping. I remember his
> saying one day, 'Old Dad,' as he called his father,
> 'have you not any wine?' Whereupon Turner senior
> produced a bottle of currant, which Turner
> smelling, said, 'Why, what you been about?'

It seems that his father had added too much gin.

Old Dad settled very happily and comfortably into Sandycombe Lodge, where he took particular pleasure in tending the garden. On Tuesdays he visited the market at Brentford, and would return with the week's provisions stored in a knotted blue handkerchief. In the spring and summer he would supervise the gallery in Harley Street, when his son was exhibiting, and often made the journey from Twickenham on foot. When Constable and Farington

wig

Turner. Sen.

D.º Jun.ᵒ

R A

Day. Jan.ʸ 27ᵗʰ. 1812.

Turner's beloved 'Old Dad'. After his mother's death in an asylum, Turner invited his father to share his home. The old man lived out the rest of his life with his son, working as his housekeeper and gardener as well as his artist's assistant. This sketch shows the father in the audience at one of the son's lectures on perspective (27 January 1812). Below are Turner's eyes.

once visited the gallery, the old man told them that 'he had walked from Twickenham this morning, eleven miles; his age, 68. In two days the last week he said he had walked fifty miles.' He might have used his son's pony, Crop-Ear, but for some reason chose not to do so. Perhaps the beast was considered to be Turner's sole possession; he rode on it for various painting expeditions, and declared that 'it would climb like a cat and never get tired'. When it died, after strangling itself on its own fastenings, he buried it in the garden.

Old Dad did in the end find an alternative mode of travelling. 'Why lookee here,' he told an acquaintance, 'I have found a way at last of coming up cheap from Twickenham to open my son's gallery. I found out the inn where the market-gardeners baited their horses; I made friends with one on 'em and now, for a glass of gin a day, he brings me up in his cart on top of the vegetables.'

The exhibition gallery in Harley Street had now been satisfactorily renovated and in 1812 Turner showed some of the paintings inspired by his journey to the West Country. But these are not simply images of a specific place or setting; they are images of radiance and pellucid space. In one of them, *Teignmouth*, a young girl watches two cows by the sea-shore; she has raised her arms above her head, in instruction or salutation, while above her the great glowing sky reaches into immensity.

The major work of this year, however, was reserved for the Royal Academy. *Snow Storm: Hannibal and his Army crossing the Alps* may have owed something to Turner's readings in classical history, but it was also a scene of great significance to what we may now call the Romantic imagination. It had been described by Mrs Radcliffe, for example, in *The Mysteries of Udolpho*. The painting was praised by critics and other artists at the time as a grand and sublime piece of work. The diarist, Crabb Robinson, believed it to be 'the most marvellous landscape I had ever seen . . . I shall never forget it'. The celebrated painter, John Flaxman, was only a little less enthusiastic and described it as 'the best painting in the Exhibition'. It is a picture of astounding power and energy, the great movement of the storm billowing across the canvas as if the paint itself were surcharged with fever and animation. The forces of the atmospheric world here far surpass the movements of men, in a paean to the natural sublime.

Chapter Seven
1813–1816

When Turner conversed with Constable in the summer of the following year, at a Royal Academy dinner, Constable reported that 'I was a good deal entertained with Turner. I always expected to find him what I did. He has a wonderful range of mind.' It is an accurate comment, despite the fact that Turner never returned the compliment; he was never fond of Constable and a fellow artist went so far as to say that Turner 'detested' him.

But the 'range' of which Constable spoke was given material expression in this year at the Academy exhibition. After the grandeur and sublimity of *Hannibal crossing the Alps* Turner submitted a painting in quite a different key. It was entitled *Frosty Morning*, depicting a man with a gun and a young girl with a hare across her shoulders in a landscape populated by labourers and horses. As in many of Turner's more naturalistic paintings, the story or narrative remains oblique and mysterious. Monet said of it that it was '*peint les yeux ouverts*'. Turner's eyes were opened in spiritual as well as material vision, with the whiteness of the beaten earth and the whiteness of the sky in implicit communion. The artist himself was characteristically matter-of-fact about the whole process, declaring that 'he was travelling by a coach in Yorkshire and sketched it en route. There is a stagecoach in the distance that he was on at the time.' It has often been claimed, at this anecdotal level, that the adult male is Walter Fawkes and that the young girl is the image of one of Turner's own illegitimate daughters.

Frosty Morning seems to have been the only newly composed oil-painting that he exhibited in 1813, the rest being selected from previous oils he had finished. The sudden dearth may have been the result of the debilitating illness that he had been suffering in the previous year, or it may simply have been the result of fatigue. His rate of production had, for many years, been extraordinary. He had also turned his attention to the production of water-colours designed for the engraver.

There was one other local difficulty which may have been a cause of some enervation. A collector and amateur artist, Sir George Beaumont, had decided that Turner was a pernicious influence upon English painting and, from a position of some authority, declaimed to the world on Turner's many sins against artistic propriety. He declared that he 'had done more harm in misleading the taste than any other artist'. He accused him, not unjustly, of 'perpetually aiming to be extraordinary'. Yet his persistent criticism angered Turner. Beaumont was an influential man, considered a possible president of the Royal Academy, and his public hostility to Turner rankled. An admirer and imitator of Turner, Augustus Callcot, had been similarly disparaged by Beaumont and had as a result sold none of his work at the Royal Academy exhibition for three years. In 1813 Turner had determined to show nothing at the Royal Academy but then, on further reflection, he decided that this would be to give Beaumont a small victory. He told

Callcot that he was 'determined not to give way before Sir George's remarks'. So *Frosty Morning* appeared upon the walls of the Academy.

In the same summer he managed to retreat from the somewhat febrile atmosphere of London and paid a second visit to Devonshire. He stayed at Plymouth, from which town he made various excursions into the surrounding countryside. A local journalist, Cyrus Redding, was fortunate enough to accompany him on some of these trips and left a record of his encounters with the now celebrated artist. He described him as a 'rather stout and bluff-looking' man who 'somewhat resembled the master of a merchant-man'. No doubt his ruddy complexion was derived from his labours in the open air. Turner was a 'good pedestrian, capable of roughing it in any mode the occasion might demand', but he was also an 'excellent sailor'. On one occasion they put out to sea with other passengers, when they encountered a heavy swell which turned 'boisterous'; Redding recalled that, while the others grew decidedly queasy, Turner 'sat in the stern sheets intently watching the sea, and not at all affected by the motion . . . when we were on the crest of a wave, he now and then articulated to myself – for we were sitting side by side – "That's fine! – fine!"'.

'Fine' in fact seems to have been his favoured compliment in any circumstance. Redding pointed out, in a house where they were staying, George Stubbs's painting of *Phaeton and the Horses of the Sun* – 'but it elicited no further remark than the monosyllable "fine"'. There were other celebrated paintings hanging in the house but 'they seemed to attract little of his attention'. Redding then suggested that 'it was not easy to judge from his manner what was passing in his mind'. He was in many respects a reticent man, not given to expressions of admiration or enthusiasm. It was part of his hatred of humbug in any form. He hated gush. In that he might be considered to be typically English. Redding also noticed that Turner could, when he pleased, 'make sound, pithy, though sometimes caustic remarks upon men and things with a fluency rarely heard from him'. He was possessed by a sound stock of good sense; he was always a good judge of 'men and things'. As a result of his close observations of the artist Redding concluded that 'beneath his homely exterior, there was a first-rate intellect'.

Turner was sketching all the time in Devon, both with pencil and with oil-paint. A local artist lent him a box of oils and he seized the opportunity to work *en plein air*. He worked very quickly, as was his custom, and another companion noted that 'Turner seemed pleased when the rapidity with which those sketches were done was talked of; for, departing from his habitual reserve in the instance of his pencil sketches, he made no difficulty of showing them'. The quickness of his hand was determined by the quickness of his eye. Redding described how the artist's glance 'seemed to command in a moment all that was novel in scenery, however extensive, which he had never before encountered. He would only make a few outlines on paper, scarcely intelligible to others.'

The fruit of those sketches emerged in a drawing of a landscape for his *Liber Studiorum* series, in the following year, and also for a number of water-colours that were to be used for other series of engravings such as *Picturesque Views of the Southern Coast of England* and *The Rivers of Devon*.

The first part of *Picturesque Views* had in fact already appeared, in January 1814, with four plates by Turner. He was becoming the most celebrated, and certainly best known, landscape artist in the country. In his work with engraving, too, he was engaged in what had become almost a second career.

His subsidiary career as a lecturer, however, seemed less certain. He was meant to deliver his latest commentaries upon the art of perspective on 3 January 1814, but somehow he managed to leave his notes and drawings in the coach that had carried him to Somerset House. How it was possible to mislay the essential papers for his task is difficult to understand. It might suggest some innate desire to get out of the engagement, but his absent-mindedness was actually well known. One mutual acquaintance wrote to another that 'he would be quite sure to lose your books, as he invariably does, more than half his baggage in every tour he makes, being the most careless personage of my acquaintance'.

Nevertheless an advertisement appeared in the *Morning Chronicle* two days later, announcing the loss and offering a reward of two guineas for the safe return of Turner's portfolio – that is, 'if brought before Thursday, afterwards only *One Pound* will be given for them at the end of the week'. This is perhaps an indication of Turner's parsimoniousness.

On the following day, 6 January, another advertisement appeared in the *Morning Chronicle* which stated that a gentleman, on hiring a hackney coach outside Somerset House, had found a large portfolio containing papers on the science of perspective. It added, perhaps with an attempt at wit, 'Should no application be made within fourteen days they will be disposed of as waste paper, being considered of little value'. The waste papers were indeed returned to the artist, and the postponed lecture was delivered a week later.

The final lecture was delivered on 7 February, on which date Turner's contribution to that year's exhibition at the British Institution was displayed. It was entitled *Appulia in Search of Appullus vide Ovid*. It arrived late, and was ostensibly designed to compete for an award in 'Historical or Poetical Composition'. But Turner seems to have submitted it to tease and annoy Sir George Beaumont, one of the most prominent patrons of the British Institution. He had executed the painting in the manner of Claude, as a rebuff to Beaumont and others who believed that he could not hope to emulate the French master. The garbled title itself seems to suggest that he was engaged in a form of practical or, rather, classical joke.

He exhibited a more celebrated example of his 'historical and poetical compositions' at the Royal Academy in the same year, with his *Dido and Aeneas*. It was a theme that fascinated and provoked him. Dido was the widow and heroine who, in Virgil's *Aeneid*, is betrayed by Aeneas; he leaves her for the sake of a greater destiny, since he and his descendants established Rome. Did Turner see some inkling of his own fate in Aeneas? Was he fated to eschew the love of women for the sake of his artistic destiny? Whatever his reasons, he returned to the theme of Dido in four separate works of art. In the composition of 1814 the shimmering city of Carthage lies behind the figures like some hallucination of classical splendour. As Hazlitt said in a newspaper review at the time, 'temples, palaces, groves and waterfalls are brought together in the richness of faery land . . . so infinite in variety and beauty are the objects which solicit attention'. It need not necessarily injure this mood of rapt attention to notice that Turner, in creating Carthage, seems in part to have copied the landscape around Plymouth. It was one of his great gifts to clothe the ordinary world with the majesty of poetry; as Dickens said of his own work upon *Bleak House*, he chose to depict the romantic side of familiar things.

Turner returned to the south coast this year – and, coincidentally, to the town where the two-year-old Dickens was even then living. In June he visited Portsmouth, in Hampshire, in order to sketch a review of the British fleet by the Prince Regent and the emperor of Russia. All forms of naval display seemed to excite him. He managed to make some brief sketches, but he did not stay for very long. He had to return to London, and the press of business that always faced him. He was never happy unless he was busily engaged. He was one of those natures who seem destined for work, and who take positive pride in their energy and industriousness.

The finest fruit of his journeys to the West Country was displayed at the Royal Academy in the following year, when *Crossing the Brook* was unveiled to the public. It is an idyllic scene in what seems to be an Italianate setting, but it is in fact that of the River Tamar in Devon. A girl sits upon a bank while another girl wades across to the other side, but the scene acquires its power and its fluency from the presence of great trees flowing about them; the natural world and the human world are rendered sacred. It is a composition of great depth and majesty, recognisably derived from Claude.

It was accompanied by a further meditation upon the legend of Dido, *Dido building Carthage*, which received much praise. It was compared with the work of Poussin and Rubens, and seemed to be a painting that 'in grandeur and beauty, Claude never equalled'. Sir George Beaumont of course disagreed. He believed *Dido building Carthage* to be 'painted in a false taste, not true to nature' and that *Crossing the Brook* 'was all of *pea-green* insipidity'. Contemporaries spoke of 'the great injury' that Beaumont was doing to him, but it is not clear that these criticisms mattered to Turner any more; he was, after all, being hailed as belonging to the company of the Old Masters.

It would be wrong, in any case, to suggest that his paintings were generally out of favour. Many prospective purchasers did come forward, but he rebuffed them. He did not want to sell much of his work, and in fact continually raised his prices in order to deter bidders. He may not have needed the money any more but, much more likely, he simply could not bear to part with them. *Frosty Morning*, *Crossing the Brook* and the two Dido paintings remained in his possession; they became part of what he called his family of pictures, built around him like some carapace in which he might hide himself. When Turner kept on raising the price of *Dido building Carthage*, from five hundred to two thousand pounds, the disgruntled prospective buyer asked: 'Why, what in the world are you going to do with the picture?' He replied – 'Be buried in it, to be sure.' The story was so widely credited that, at the time of his funeral, the dean of St Paul's said: 'I will not read the service over him if he is wrapped up in that picture.'

There was after all something irreligious, almost pagan, in being enveloped in a painting – especially one which celebrated the ambition of a legendary queen. Yet the theme of Dido remained close to him. The painting itself is a wonderful evocation of magnificence not untouched by mystery and melancholy. The subtitle of the painting, 'The Rise of the Carthaginian Empire', necessarily anticipates the fall and decay of Carthage at the hands of Rome; the glow of the sun upon the water casts a tranquil light upon the scene. Turner confessed later that he regarded this work as his master-piece, and is reported to have turned down the sum of five thousand guineas for it. He had determined to leave it to the nation together with the rest of his 'family' of his most treasured works.

Most of them did in fact remain in his studio until his death, as a constant reminder of his achievement. They were not always treated with the care and attention that they deserved, however. Ruskin noted that a chunk of sky had fallen out of *Crossing the Brook*, and was lying on the floor of Turner's gallery. 'What does it matter?' the artist said. 'The only use of the thing is to recall the impression.' *Dido building Carthage* suffered a similar fate, and was found in his gallery 'all mildewed and flaking off'. He hoarded his work as if it were buried treasure, but the treasure was himself. He could not bear to part with his paintings because they were an aspect of his being. When he recalled 'the impression' he was also recalling the rapt mood of attention and enchantment with which he began any particular work. These paintings were a history of his inward life, and he did not particularly care how they fared in the exterior world of change and decay.

In the summer of this year, 1815, he travelled to Farnley Hall once more to stay with Walter Fawkes and his family. He seems to have visited the household in the grouse season, when he could take up a gun, but he also employed his time by making various painting expeditions in the neighbourhood. He may have made the journey in part because he was growing tired of Sandycombe Lodge. He told a friend that he was beginning to regret the investment

Turner's Gallery: the artist showing his work, drawn from memory by his friend George Jones in 1852. Turner could not bear to part with his favourite paintings, and still hanging on the far wall is *Dido building Carthage* (see colour section).

he had made in it, and that 'Sandycombe sounds just now in my ears as an act of folly, when I reflect how little I have been able to be there this year'. It is the complaint of all those who are fortunate enough to own two homes; one house always seems to eat up the money, and never to get properly used. He also mentioned the fact that 'Daddy seems as much plagued with weeds as I am with disappointments', which suggests that the burden of horticulture was getting too strong for a man now in his seventieth year. The house also seems to have suffered from dampness, and the elderly William Turner was forever catching cold.

In this year Turner was as usual engaged in the routine business of the Royal Academy, attending meetings and partaking in dinners, supervising elections and awarding premiums to promising students. But he had also been appointed as 'Visitor' or supervisor of students in the Life class. He was never the most articulate of teachers but his instruction seems to have been of some benefit. One of his erstwhile pupils recalled that he specialised in

> a few indistinct words, a wave of the hand, a poke
> in the side, pointing at the same time to some part
> of the student's drawing, but saying nothing more
> than a 'humph!' or 'what's that for?' Yet the fault
> hinted at, the thing to be altered was there, if you
> could but find it out; and if, after a deep puzzle, you
> did succeed in comprehending his meaning, he
> would congratulate you when he came round
> again, and would give you some further hint; if not,
> he would leave you with another disdainful growl,

> or perhaps seize your porte-crayon, or with his
> broad thumb, make you at once sensible of your
> fault.

This suggests very well his practical approach to teaching. It was not a matter of principles but of demonstration. He left it to the student. He said at the end of one of his lectures on perspective that 'After all I have been saying to you, gentlemen – the theories I have explained and the rules I have laid down – you will find no better teachers than your own eyes, if used aright to see things as they are.' When a pupil asked him, 'How?' he characteristically replied, 'Suppose you *look*.'

He also introduced a novel procedure in the Life class which suggests his practicality. He would pose a live model beside an antique cast, placing him or her in the same action and attitude as the sculpture itself. The student could then observe the difference between nature and art in the most intimate and overt manner. As one student put it, 'It showed at once how much the antique sculptors had refined nature; which, if in parts it looked more beautiful than the *selected* form which is called *ideal*, as a whole looked common and vulgar by its side.' It was an enterprising approach, and demonstrates the originality of Turner's mind. His instruction does in fact seem to have been popular as well as effective. One pupil recalled that 'the schools were usually better attended during his visitorships than during those of most other members'.

One younger contemporary also recalls him saying: 'First of all, respect your paper! Keep your corners quiet. Centre your interest. And always remember that as you can never reach the *brilliancy* of nature, you need never be afraid to put your brightest light next to your deepest shadow in the *centre*, but not in the *corners* of your picture.'

It was good technical advice but his more elaborate reflections on painting can be found in some marginal notes he scrawled in a copy of John Opie's *Lectures On Painting*. Opie had written of the need for perseverance and determination in the painter's vocation, to which sound advice Turner added the comment that true achievement could only be gained with 'that power that gathers greatness as it passes' and 'an innate power that enforces, that inspires'. Here he seems to be reflecting upon his own capacities, with the recognition of some inward strength that moved him forward through the world. He also alluded to his own practice in another marginal annotation, to the effect that 'he that has the ruling enthusiasm which accompanies abilities cannot look superficially. Every glance is a glance for study . . .' The fruit of this precept can be seen in the hundreds, even thousands, of drawings which he completed on his multifarious journeys.

He was once more exhibiting at the Royal Academy in the following year, 1816, where he hung *The Temple of Jupiter Panellenius Restored* and *View of the Temple of Jupiter Panellenius, in the Island of Aegina*. On the face of it these are puzzling choices. The first shows the temple in pristine form, and the second depicts the same temple in ruins. But they both provide evidence of Turner's wish to connect his painting with the life of the larger public world. '*Panellenius*' means 'all of Greece' and in these works Turner was expressing his sympathy with the movement of

Greek liberation to which Lord Byron had also attached himself. There is perhaps a sorrowful reminder that modern Greece itself had fallen into decay and desuetude, but the general mood is one of homage and celebration. The depiction of the ancient temple 'restored' was also a token of the restoration of liberty in Greece itself. The second painting also demonstrates Turner's abiding interest in archaeology, a pursuit that had become something of a 'craze' in the early nineteenth century.

But good intentions do not necessarily make good art. Ruskin, Turner's most eloquent supporter, consigned both works to a list of 'nonsense pictures', and in a periodical essay William Hazlitt criticised them as 'a combination of gaudy hues'. He wrote more in sorrow than in anger, however, believing that Turner had for some reason abused his 'great genius'. That he was in other respects an acute commentator upon Turner's work is attested by an article which he wrote earlier that year in the *Examiner*. Of Turner's landscape paintings Hazlitt wrote that 'they are pictures of the elements of air, earth, and water. The artist delights to go back to the first chaos of the world . . . All is without form and void. Some one said of his landscapes that they were *pictures of nothing, and very like.*'

It should be recalled that these words were written before any of Turner's later works had been revealed to the world, when his experiments with light might well suggest 'pictures of nothing'. That such a description could be applied to him, so relatively early in the course of his development, is an indication of how truly revolutionary he already seemed to his contemporaries. Paintings like *Frosty Morning* and *Crossing the Brook*, which seem now to be natural and

Two portraits of Turner:
The Self-Portrait (circa 1799)
is probably an idealised image
of the young romantic; whereas the
elderly *Turner on Varnishing Day*
(by S. W. Parrott, circa 1846) is full
of character and inscribed 'from life'.

Snow Storm: Hannibal and his Army Crossing the Alps (1812) contrasted
with *Frosty Morning* (1813). The first is an example of the sublime grandeur of
nature and of Turner's interest in the Carthaginians; the second is a homely scene in
which the girl is said to be modelled on Turner's illegitimate daughter, Evelina,
and one of the horses on his own pony, Crop-Ear.

Dido Building Carthage, exhibited at the Academy in 1815.
Turner regarded this as his masterpiece and is reputed to have turned down 5000 guineas for it; it was still in his studio at the time of his death. He returned to the subject of Dido in four separate works of art.

Lord Egremont greeted by his nine dogs (on the left of the picture).
Petworth Park: Tillington Church in the Distance, circa 1828, was painted by Turner as
art of a set for the Grinling Gibbons dining room at Petworth. Turner's two loyal patrons,
Lord Egremont and Walter Fawkes, also became his well-loved friends, and he was a
welcome guest in their houses, Farnley Hall in Yorkshire and Petworth Park in Sussex.

Turner was an adventurous traveller.
(*Facing page, above*) When he crossed the Channel for the first time, he was
'nearly swampt' on arrival. The resulting *Calais Pier* was exhibited in 1803.
(*Below*) *Messieurs les Voyageurs.* Turner (in top-hat in foreground) 'bivouaced in the
snow with fires lighted for 3 hours on Mont Tarate while the diligence was righted
and dug out, for a Bank of Snow saved it from upsetting'. 22 January 1829,
during his second visit to Italy.

When sketching in Scotland as a guest of Walter Scott, Turner insisted on
entering Fingal's Cave on a stormy day. 'It is not very pleasant or safe when the wave
is right in.' His host did not accompany him. *Staffa, Fingal's Cave* (1832), which today
is considered a masterpiece of sea and sky, did not find a purchaser for thirteen
years; the buyer reputedly complained that it was 'indistinct'.

The Battle of Trafalgar (1824) was a commission from the King. Turner worked on it for 16 months, but it found favour neither with George IV nor William IV, and was banished to Greenwich. Turner believed that this failure cost him a knighthood.

One of the masterpieces of Turner's later years: *The Fighting Temeraire* (1838) – 'the art of colour itself taken to the highest possible pitch'.

familiar enough, appeared at the time to be shockingly new. It is an indication, at least, of the speed with which artistic developments are assimilated.

He did not exhibit any works at his own gallery this year, in part because he was busily engaged on other projects, and in the summer of 1816 he travelled again to Yorkshire. He had been engaged 'to make drawings for a History of Yorkshire', according to Farington, for a price of three thousand guineas. Since he was commissioned to complete 120 drawings in all, the purchase of each drawing for twenty-five guineas does not seem unreasonable. The engraver received between sixty and eighty guineas for completing each plate. The project was abandoned, however, as it over-ran on costs. He finished twenty drawings for a *History of Richmondshire*, and that was the end of it.

While in Yorkshire he stayed once more at Farnley Hall with Walter Fawkes, but he wandered much further afield to Leeds, Doncaster and Grantham. He took a horse and rode over the Stake Pass, across Redmire Moor; he rode from Richmond to Barnard Castle and then crossed the Fells. He must have been an expert, not to say indefatigable, horseman. On one stage of this journey he wrote to a friend, 'weather miserably wet; I shall be web-foot, like a Drake – excepting the curled feather – but I must proceed Northward – adieu'. While battling across the Fells in the wild weather, through coarse heather and peat, it seems that he almost lost his life. He recorded that he could only manage eleven miles in nine hours.

But on the course of these long and arduous rides through Yorkshire he had managed to complete some 450 drawings. It had been worth the peril.

There is one anecdote of this Yorkshire journey which bears repetition. Apparently he brought a sealed letter of introduction from his London publishers, Longman, to a Leeds bookseller by the name of Robinson. In this confidential missive Messrs Longman informed Robinson that 'above all things remember that Turner is a GREAT JEW'. They were perhaps referring to his financial acumen, but Robinson interpreted the description literally. He suspected that Turner would not wish to attend church on Sunday, and apologised when serving him ham for dinner. If Turner had discovered the truth of this situation, eventually described by his first biographer George Walter Thornbury, he would no doubt have been more amused than annoyed.

He returned to Farnley in time for the opening of the grouse season and a family tragedy: in the course of the shooting, Walter Fawkes's younger brother was injured and subsequently died.

Chapter Eight
1816–1819

Turner had worked on drawing and painting the English landscape for some twenty-five years, ever since he had travelled to Bristol in the autumn of 1791 at the age of sixteen. He had created a panorama of England in succeeding years, an achievement that was then more associated with him in the public mind than his more controversial paintings. But he had not been entirely insular – he had travelled to France and Switzerland, for example, in 1802 – and by the end of 1816 he began making plans for a European journey in the succeeding year. It was to be one of many visits to the European continent, in the course of which Turner would reflect upon the role and nature of his own painting and upon his virtues as a specifically English artist.

He showed only one painting at the Royal Academy this year, but it was one that provoked much admiring comment. It was entitled *The Decline of the Carthaginian Empire* – the full title is some fifty-one words long – and it acts as a companion piece to his painting of two years before on the subject of Dido erecting the city of Carthage itself. Its appearance prompted one critic to call for the establishment of a 'National Gallery' where such works could be hung beside the Old Masters. The livid sky and the setting sun were also the occasions for praise, as if Turner were depicting the fiery splendour of an expiring age. He had already advanced the art of history painting to new intensity and even sublimity, as if the poetry of Byron or of Shelley had found colour and texture, light and shadow.

Then, in the summer of 1817, he set off by boat from Margate to Ostend. He had made a preparatory list of indispensable items, as many travellers do. He included in it books and fever medicine as well as pencils and colours. He also made out a list of Dutch phrases with their translation in English – 'what church do you call it; can I leave my mantle; have you seen my baggage'. The last question became of vital importance. Inevitably he managed to lose his knapsack, which held a waistcoat, a razor, six cravats, and a guide-book to Belgium.

While *en route* he also made notes to himself on his circumstances. In Ostend, for example, he wrote: 'inn The Hotel de la Cour Imperiale. Badly served. Charges dear. 2 francs for Breakfast . . .' He travelled by carriage through Ghent and Brussels, and then spent a day inspecting the site of the battle of Waterloo. Here he made notes of the battlefield, which evidently still bore signs of the recent slaughter, with ashy cinders of the bodies as well as blood-stains on the farm walls and buildings. He jotted down the notes of fatalities, '1500 killed here' and '4000 killed here'.

He went on to Cologne since his principal object was to make a series of pencil sketches of the Rhine which were later worked up into water-colours for Walter Fawkes. He walked for some forty miles, but then took a boat to Mainz before returning to Cologne. Then he went on to Antwerp, where the work of Rubens was to be seen in its most appropriate surroundings, and then to Rotterdam and Amsterdam where he had reminded himself to see Rembrandt's *Night Watch* and *The Anatomy Lesson*.

On his return to England he travelled north once more. He spent some time at Raby Castle in County Durham, at the invitation of the third earl of Darlington who commissioned him to depict his country seat. The work duly appeared, and was exhibited at the Royal Academy before being despatched to its owner, complete with a fox-hunting scene. The hounds are to be seen racing across the billowing landscape. It was at Raby Castle that he completed the water-colours of the Rhineland which were purchased by Fawkes. He had taken three sketchbooks with him on his journey, and out of these he made some fifty-one water-colours. But the transformation was complete. The pencil drawings were executed rapidly and sketch out the topo-graphical details of the scene; only later, in the completed water-colours, did he impart atmosphere and colour.

The more formal results of his journey were exhibited in the Royal Academy in 1818 with *Dort, or Dordrecht, the Dort Packet-Boat from Rotterdam becalmed* and *The Field of Waterloo*. The *Dort* painting was reputed to be one of Turner's own favourites, and indeed much of the comment at the time was laudatory. The *Morning Chronicle* described it as 'one of the most magnificent pictures ever exhibited' which 'does honour to the age'. More graphically, perhaps, a fellow artist described its colours as so vivid that 'it almost puts your eyes out'. It is indeed a magnificent piece, with the stately sailing boat resting calmly on the water and casting shadows upon the serene surface so that it seems almost to be hovering in air. It is said that another artist gave up his own place so that it could be exhibited in a central position in the Great Room of the Academy; if so, it was a tribute to the respect with which Turner's work was now greeted. Constable declared of the painting that it was 'I think the most complete work of genius I ever saw.'

The calm and composure of this painting are amply contrasted by the glare and horror of *The Field of Waterloo* in which the thousands of dead lie mixed upon the plain of battle. Behind the scene of fallen men is the fervid glare of burning buildings, sending up billows of black smoke into the already fiery and super-charged air. It is not necessarily a paean against warfare as such – in some respects Turner was a profound patriot and would not have regretted the result of the battle – but rather a description of the lamentable effects of human strife. It shows the pity of victory, against a background which has intimations of eternity.

The wife of Walter Fawkes made an entry in her diary for Thursday 4 June 1818. 'Went to Eton to see the boat-race. Dined and slept at Salt Hill. Little Turner came with us.' And little Turner used the excursion to great effect by finishing a sepia drawing of 'Windsor Castle from Salt Hill'. His landscape work was still flourishing, with many water-colours issuing from his brush for the engraver's burin.

In the autumn he travelled to Scotland, since he had agreed to furnish drawings for *The Provincial Antiquities of Scotland*; Sir Walter Scott had consented to write the text for this volume, but their eventual encounter was not a success. Some months later Scott wrote to a friend that 'Turner's palm is as itchy as his fingers are ingenious and he will, take my word for it, do nothing without cash and anything for it. He is almost the only man of genius I ever knew who is sordid in these matters.' The cause of Scott's complaint is likely to have been Turner's determination to be paid the highest possible fees for his work. But why should he not assert his own worth? Scott, of all people, should have known the value of money in return for creative labour.

Turner also met certain Scottish artists, as befitted a visiting celebrity. But his manner did not altogether please his generous hosts. A sister of one artist wrote to an acquaintance that 'we are all, however, provoked at the coldness of his manner. We intended to have a joyous evening on his arrival, but finding him such a *stick*, we did not think the pleasure of showing him to our friends would be adequate to the trouble and expense.'

Turner was only ever a 'stick' in the 'wrong' company. It may be that there was some incompatibility of temperament between the English painter and his Scottish hosts. There is some indication that he was not in any case in the best of moods. A dinner had been arranged for him, with ten guests, and he failed to turn up. He may have found the welcomes just too hearty.

His interest in 'cash', intimated by Scott, was in fact put to some beneficial use in this year. In the summer of 1818 he had purchased three adjacent parcels of land in Twickenham, and in his will he instructed his executors to build alms-houses on them for the benefit of impoverished artists. Since he was so secretive about financial matters, his motives were often misconstrued. Questions of finance must certainly have influenced his decision, at the very beginning of the following year, to discontinue the series known as *Liber Studiorum*. He had supervised its publication but he had had neither the time nor the inclination to publish it punctually; he had also had disagreements with various engravers, and had clearly decided that he had had enough of the entire business. His new manner of working, producing water-colours for other publishers, was more efficacious and more remunerative.

His reputation was in any case greatly enhanced in the early spring when there were two separate exhibitions of his work. Sir John Leicester exhibited eight of his oil-paintings, housed in his gallery in Hill Street, and a month later Walter Fawkes displayed no less than seventy of Turner's water-colours in the rooms of his town house in Grosvenor Place. It was a remarkable collection in the most obvious sense, since Turner's water-colours had never been seen before as a coherent whole. One newspaper wrote that 'this artist's fame can acquire no better vindication than this Collection', and added with a touch of jingoism that Turner was 'at the head of all English (and in saying so we necessarily include all living) artists'.

At the Royal Academy in 1819 he chose to display two oil-paintings, *Entrance of the Meuse: Orange-Merchant on the Bar, going to Pieces* and *England: Richmond Hill, on the Prince Regent's Birthday*. The first was obviously indebted to his recent journey to the Low Countries, and was the first painting by Turner ever to be seen by the visionary artist Samuel Palmer. Palmer was fourteen years old at the time and later recalled that 'being by nature a lover of smudginess, I have revelled in him from that day to this'.

If the Meuse painting is the result of a recent journey, the oil of Richmond Hill returns to one of his old obsessions. It also has the distinction of being the largest work he had yet completed, some eleven feet in length. It can be viewed as an affirmation of nationhood or as a celebration of the royal family (it has been suggested that Turner was in pursuit of royal patronage), but it can also be seen as part of a tribute to himself at the centre of the landscape tradition. His residence, Sandycombe Lodge, is situated in the middle of the composition as if his was a secret presence in this fluent and melodious work. But such paintings go beyond conscious intention or motive. Richmond seems for him to have become a sacred place, part of the landscape of his imagination. There were certain regions of the Thames that prompted in him the most profound meditations or, rather, his response to the riverscape had within it elements of rapture as well as contemplation.

There is a description of Turner visiting the exhibition put on by Walter Fawkes in Grosvenor Place. He came alone and

> while he leaned on the centre table in the great room, or slowly worked his rough way through the mass, he attracted every eye in the brilliant crowd, and seemed to me like a victorious Roman general, the principal figure in his own triumph. Perhaps no British artist ever retired from an exhibition of his own works, with so much reason for unmixed satisfaction, or more genuine proofs of well deserved admiration from the public.

He did indeed have every reason for 'unmixed satisfaction'.

Chapter Nine
1819–1827

It seems that he was now ready to confront Italy, then considered to be the world's home of painting. His enthusiasm for the Italian landscape may already have been kindled by some water-colours of Italian scenes which he had just completed, using as his models certain *camera lucida* sketches by James Hakewill; Turner's work would eventually be seen in a volume entitled *Tour in Italy*. A letter from a fellow artist, Sir Thomas Lawrence, had stated that 'Turner should come to Rome. His genius would be here supplied with materials, and entirely congenial with it.' Turner himself no doubt would have agreed since a few weeks later, at the beginning of August 1819, he set off across the Channel on his way to Italy.

He journeyed to Turin by way of Paris, Lyons and Grenoble. From Turin he travelled to Como and the lakes of the vicinity before moving on to Milan and Verona. And then he encountered Venice for the first time. His first thoughts on seeing the floating city are not recorded but we may imagine the response of one who was so deeply attuned to the movement of water, to the passage of light and the intermingling of the sun among the waves. This was a marine world of boats and barques and gondolas, of masts and sails and flags of every colour and description; it was a world of great ships and wide quays, with palaces and domed churches seeming to spring out of the sea itself. There were boats of dark hue lying in the shadows, the reflections of lamps and houses and torches glistening in the water, arches and mansions and towers innumerable. There were grand piazzas, too, with candle lights like something out of an enchanted fable; there were porches and cloisters and galleries falling away in an endless perspective. This was Turner's world.

It was perhaps his world in a different sense also. The connection between Venice and England has often been made, both insular and maritime powers of uncertain or perilous destiny. But there was perhaps a closer connection. David Wilkie, the artist whose work had recently hung on the walls of the Royal Academy beside that of Turner, remarked of Venice that 'by land and by water the town is full of intricacy, full of St Martin's Courts, of Maiden Lanes, and Cranbourne Alleys, interrupted at every corner with canals and high bridges'. Of course Turner's boyhood haunts had been Maiden Lane and Cranbourne Alley, now transposed into the setting of water and of the sea. How could he fail to fall half in love with such a place?

He stayed for only five days on this occasion but the city seized his imagination; he filled some 160 pages of his sketchbooks with drawings and groups of drawings. He also executed some wonderful water-colours of the Venetian morning, where the translucent and ethereal light of the city is evoked in washes of blue and yellow. That sense of light never left him. It irradiates much of the rest of his work. His oil-paintings of Venice, completed at a later date, glow upon the wall as if a bright light were shining through them. The effect of Venice upon him was altogether profound, and seemed to grow in intensity as the years passed. His various periods of stay in Venice lasted altogether for less than four weeks, but in the last twenty years of his painting life he devoted one third of his productive work to views of that city. For him it became a jewel of great price.

From Venice he made a slow progress to Rome, in which city he arrived towards the end of October. He stayed there until approximately the middle of December, during which time he completed some fifteen hundred pencil sketches. He had come to see, and to draw, the city and its landscape hallowed for him by many associations with Raphael and Claude. He drew everything – columns, fascias, entablatures, pillars, ruins and inscriptions. He studied paintings and sculptures in the Corsini and Farnese palaces; he visited the churches and the chapels; he walked among the temples and the markets of ancient Rome.

He was not continuously in the Italian capital, however, since some timely activity from Vesuvius prompted him to travel on to Naples. In an era without the benefit of cheap cameras, one aspect of the artist's role was to record the spectacle of great events. The son of Sir John Soane happened to be in the vicinity, and wrote in a letter home that

> Turner is in the neighbourhood of Naples making rough pencil sketches to the astonishment of the Fashionables, who wonder of what use these rough draughts can be – simple souls! At Rome a sucking blade of the brush made the request of going out

with pig Turner to colour – he grunted for an
answer that it would take too much time to colour
in the open air – he could make 15 or 16 pencil
sketches to one coloured, and then grunted his way
home.

The 'sucking blade of the brush' was one of those English
amateurs or dilettanti who thronged to Italy to satisfy their
finer feelings and also to pick up relatively cheap tuition
from Italian professionals. Turner despised such people, and
his 'grunt' was no doubt distinctive.

He also made a private pilgrimage, to the grave of Virgil
outside Naples. Virgil was for him the poet who had
managed to combine the pastoral and the allegorical, to
create spiritual landscapes, and to derive legendary enchantment out of historical events. In his own way, and in his own
medium, he had similar ambitions.

He returned home by way of Turin and the Mont Cenis
Pass, where the snow was so deep that his carriage capsized.
Turner, and the rest of the passengers, were obliged to climb
out through the window and complete the rest of the
journey by foot – or, as he put it later, 'flounder up to our
knees, nothing less, in snow all the way down . . .' A fight
broke out between the guides and drivers which no doubt
finished as quickly as it had started. But Turner was as
observant as he was self-possessed. He completed a water-
colour for Walter Fawkes, entitled *The Passage of Mt. Cenis,
15th Jany, 1820*, which amid the sublime white landscape of
the Alps conjures up all the details of the incident.

There were of course other fruits of his Italian journey. By
dint of effort and hard work he managed to complete one

large oil-painting for the Royal Academy exhibition of 1820. It was entitled *Rome from the Vatican: Raffaelle, accompanied by La Fornarina, preparing his pictures for the decoration of the Loggia*. It was a densely allusive title – 'La Fornarina' being the mistress of Raphael – and the picture itself is somewhat difficult to decipher. It is not one of Turner's happier compositions, being both cluttered and anachronistic. It has been suggested that the painting is in part semi-autobiographical, but there is no reason to doubt Turner's responsiveness to Rome and the Roman landscape.

From the time of his return at the beginning of 1820 he was engaged in Academy business, and indeed in this year he was appointed inspector of the Cast Collection. He was also obliged to serve on various committees, determining matters from pensions to purchasing policies. At a later date he was also appointed auditor of the Academy, which suggests that his reputation for the cautious handling of money had spread among his colleagues. There is no doubt that he was in fact a good member of any committee, being brisk and expeditious in all matters of business.

He was also concerned with matters of property. On the death of his uncle this year he inherited two houses in Wapping and some land in Barking; it is a testimony to his entrepreneurial skills that he converted the pair of houses into a single public house called the Ship and Bladebone. It was not perhaps the most unusual title for a public house by the riverside, but it conformed to his London instincts. In the same period he was involved in litigation with one of his tenants, a dentist renting rooms in his house in Harley Street.

*

But his most important concern this year was the building of
a new gallery; he was also involved with the enlargement and
remodelling of the house in Queen Anne Street. He wrote
to a friend to thank him

> for your kind offer of refuge to the Houseless,
> which in the present instance is humane . . . some
> demon eclypt Mason, Bricklayer, Carpenter etc.
> etc. etc. has kept me in constant oscillation between
> Twickenham and London, from London to Twit
> [sic], that I have found the art of going about doing
> nothing – 'so out of nothing, nothing can come'.

'Doing nothing' here meant having neither the time nor the
opportunity to paint which, for an artist of Turner's energy,
was perhaps the most aggravating condition of all. Yet he
managed to channel his activity into the new house itself.
He busied himself about its architectural details, and made
elaborate plans for the furnishing of his new residence.

The work on the house was extensive, and continued well
into the next year; the consequent disturbance meant that
Turner had no paintings to exhibit in the Academy show of
1821. One artistic colleague told Farington that Turner had
received no commissions, but had added that 'he can do
very well without any commissions'. By which he meant that
Turner was by now sufficiently wealthy to be able to dis-
pense with ready money. One of the sources of his income
was on display this year, however, since in the spring of 1821
there was an exhibition of the work of engravers, many of
whom had created prints out of Turner's water-colours.
One reviewer particularly remarked that 'the prints of W.B.

and G. Cooke after Turner are remarkable for brilliancy, spirited and scientific etching, airiness, depth and power'.

Yet some critics have also discerned in this pause, this cessation of painterly activity, an instinctive change in his art. It was as if he were taking breath before embarking upon a new engagement with the possibilities of colour in his work. Certainly, by 1824, there is a renewed emphasis upon what one contemporary described as 'the mysteries of light' in Turner's pictures together with 'the singular mixture of prismatic colours with which he represents sky and water'. It may have been connected with his Italian journey, and perhaps more particularly to his immersion in the light of Venice, but it can more plausibly be attached to the inherent development of his genius. He was beginning to create what might be called structures of colour or even structures of light, which in themselves create harmony and contrast, recession and movement. His contemporaries sometimes referred to it as painted mist but it is rather the depiction of the mysterious intimations of evolving form.

The new gallery was opened with a flourish in 1822. It was situated on the first floor of the house, beside Turner's studio; on the ground floor were the parlour and the dining-room, which seem to have betrayed little other than the artist's opulent circumstances. The whole ménage was supervised by Hannah Danby, the niece of his erstwhile mistress, who stayed with her employer until his death. There have been many descriptions of the gallery itself, and one early visitor recalled that the walls were of the colour then known as 'Indian Red'. He went on to say that it was the best lighted gallery I have ever seen, and the effect got by the simplest means; a herring net was spread from end to end just above the walls, and sheets of tissue spread on the net, the roof itself being like that of a greenhouse. By this the light was diffused close to the pictures.

Stories of Turner's gallery abound, making it sound like a cross between Aladdin's cave and Bluebeard's castle.

It did not for long remain in its pristine state. When one artist called in the 1840s, during a day of heavy London rain, he found 'the floor strewed with old saucers, basins and dishes, placed there to catch the rain, which poured from broken panes, cracks and crevices'. Many of the paintings were cracked and peeling; others were used to keep open doors or to block a window. They were dusty and dirty, stained and altogether neglected.

Another painter, William Leighton Leitch, was invited to visit the gallery when Turner was not present, apparently a rare privilege. Leitch noticed at once that the house in Queen Anne Street 'had a desolate look. The door was shabby and nearly destitute of paint and the windows were obscured by dirt.' On ringing the bell

the door was opened a very little bit, and a very singular figure appeared behind it. It was a woman covered from head to foot with dingy whitish flannel, her face being nearly hidden. She did not speak, so I told her my name, and that Mr Turner had given me permission to see the pictures. I gave her my card and a piece of silver with it, on which she pointed to the stair and to a door at the head of it, but she never spoke a word and shutting the door she disappeared.

Hannah Danby was the presiding spirit of this forlorn place; she hid her face because she was suffering from some debilitating and disfiguring skin disease.

When Leitch sat down in a chair, the better to view a particular painting, he suddenly felt something moving around his neck. It was a cat. In his alarm he startled four or five more cats that had begun to creep around his legs. He fled in horror, and 'on looking back I saw the cats at the top glaring at me, and I noticed that every one of them was without a tail'. The cats were of course Manx, and it has often been said that cats without tails save money; they do not take so long to enter or exit a room, and so preserve its heat.

It is a cautionary tale of entering the great artist's sanctum, but not as cautionary as if the artist himself had been present. Turner's studio was adjacent to the gallery, and he had fitted a spy-hole so that he could see exactly what the visitors were doing in his apparent absence. If they attempted to touch a painting – or, worse, to sketch it – he came out in belligerent mood. One man dared to make a note of a painting; Turner came out and tore it up. Very few visitors were allowed to enter the studio itself which harboured the *secreta secretorum* of Turner's art. It was what W.H. Auden called in another context the cave of making, and for Turner it was very like a cave – a secret and secluded place where he could work and brood. Here he kept on a shelf several glass bottles, each one filled with a different colour – among them chrome yellow, emerald green and red lead. There were many brushes, small and large, a bureau of old paints and oils, and a palette upon which he mixed the variously coloured powders with cold-drawn oil. In the studio, too, he kept models of ships and some views of foreign scenery. Here he worked from early morning, keeping long hours, and yet 'work' is hardly the word for what was essentially a mode of life. From here emerged the painting hung in the Royal Academy exhibition of 1822, *What You Will!*, a study of a scene from *Twelfth Night*; the title itself has a punning allusion to Watteau, whose style he seems to have borrowed for the occasion. It is very much a studio piece, with various Shakespearian characters grouped among statuary and trees.

If he was essentially a studio painter he still made his forays into the world in order to refresh his imagination and to find new themes. In the summer of this year, for example, he travelled up to Edinburgh in order to record the arrival there of George IV. It has been suggested that this was a bid for royal approval or patronage near the start of a new reign (George had been crowned two years before), or that he was preparing for a series of royal paintings, but the latter endeavour came to nothing. Four unfinished oil-paintings of this royal visit were later found in his studio. But he always made good use of his time. That is why he found the opportunity on this journey to sketch various rivers and ports, in preparation for a book of engravings on that subject.

Even if he had not succeeded in inaugurating a series of royal paintings, it seems that he had caught the new king's notice. At the end of 1822 George IV commissioned Turner to paint the battle of Trafalgar, to be placed in one of the state apartments of St James's Palace. He must have seemed the ideal artist for such an enterprise. He readily complied, and wrote to the king's marine painter for details of the ships that took part in the naval action. He worked upon the canvas for some sixteen months and, as a result of his labours, had nothing to offer the Royal Academy for its exhibition in 1824.

In the spring of that year *The Battle of Trafalgar* was revealed to the world, gaining a decidedly mixed response. It was generally believed that the government was not happy with the completed work, and that the scene depicted was implausible and inaccurate. He had received the benefit of professional advice, however, during the last stages of its composition. While finishing it in St James's Palace he was 'instructed daily by the naval men about the Court. During the eleven days he altered the rigging to suit the fancy of every fresh critic; and he did it with the greatest good humour.' He was not in 'good humour', however, on the day he was approached by the duke of Clarence, later to become William IV. Turner seems to have been somewhat belligerent and the Duke ended the conversation by saying, 'I have been at sea the greater part of my life, sir, you don't know who you are talking to and I'll be damned if you know what you are talking about.' This sounds apocryphal – who, after all, would have reported the exchange? – but the painting was not received with royal favour. It was banished to Greenwich, and may have cost Turner the knighthood which he believed he deserved.

He was perhaps more fortunate in the reception of his water-colours at an exhibition arranged by the engraver

W.B. Cooke, in Soho Square. Fifteen of Turner's works were hung here, confirming his mastery of that medium. In 1824, too, he began preparing for a series of landscapes of England and Wales; for that series, and perhaps for earlier ones, he had now devised a technique of painting water-colours in batches. Sometimes he would paint the subject on several different sheets, adding and refining until one of them caught the mood and atmosphere that he required. On other occasions it seems that he would employ just one colour on several different compositions before turning to another colour. There was another technique that one artist saw him using.

> There were four drawing boards, each of which had a handle screwed to the back. Turner, after sketching in his subject in a fluent manner, grasped the handle and plunged the whole drawing into a pail of water by his side. Then quickly he washed in the principal hues that he required, flowing tint into tint, until this stage of the work was complete. Leaving the first drawing to dry, he took the second board and repeated the operation. By the time the fourth drawing was laid in, the first would be ready for the finishing touches.

It was an interesting technique, perhaps owing something to the factory system that was even then expanding all over England but of course also conforming to Turner's own brisk and expeditious nature.

In this period, too, he was arranging and labelling his

sketchbooks so that they might form some kind of order. He put numbers on the spines, as well as compiling a table of contents, so that he had ready access to the thousands of landscape drawings that he had executed over the preceding years. It was part of the tidiness and efficiency with which he approached all aspects of his life and work, but he may also have been putting in order his entire corpus in anticipation of his eventual demise. He had an overwhelming need to leave his legacy to posterity in as complete a form as possible.

He employed four of these sketchbooks on a tour in the summer of 1824, when he travelled to the rivers Meuse and Mosel. In one of these books he appended little diagrams of the areas he was visiting, complete with miles, local inns and important 'sights'. He was away for a little over a month, and in that period completed many thousands of sketches. Two of these sketchbooks were expressly designed for the artistic traveller; they were soft-covered, and could be rolled up in order to be stowed in a capacious coat-pocket. He travelled for much of the time in a boat or in a barge pulled by horses; there are notations such as 'horses obliged to swim' and 'horses again across the river'. He also travelled by road, of course, although on one occasion his 'diligence' or coach overturned and had to be dug out of a ditch between Ghent and Brussels. He completed a water-colour of that incident. He sketched everything, his capacious eye taking in scenes and landscapes at a glance – the churches, the bridges, the mountains, the castles, the villages, the inns and the medieval buildings he glimpsed *en route*. Only one oil-painting was actually created out of the materials of this journey, *Harbour of Dieppe (Changement de Domicile)*, which was exhibited at the Royal Academy in the following year.

On its presentation in 1825 it was praised in one periodical as 'one of those magnificent works of art, which make us proud of the age we live in'. Other critics were not so sure, and complained that the painting was not 'true to nature'; the brilliancy of its colours, and the general heightening of light and tone, were not consonant with what the English knew of Dieppe. He had given the French port the atmosphere of Venice. It is clear enough that most observers had not yet understood the direction of Turner's art, or the qualities that he was now bringing to it. They were happier with his water-colours and, indeed, with the engravings of those water-colours. Such works were more familiar.

Turner must have been satisfied with the results of his expedition to the Meuse and the Mosel since, in the late August of this year, he travelled to Holland before proceeding up the Rhine. He was revisiting the landscapes of the Dutch masters he revered. He visited The Hague as well as Amsterdam and Antwerp, Ghent and Bruges. His methods were much the same as those of the previous year, with sketchbooks on hand for brief notations and more elaborate drawings. Out of this trip came one of his most famous paintings, although it had little to do with the topography of Holland itself. It was entitled *Cologne: The Arrival of a Packet Boat, Evening*, and derived from an impression he received at the very end of the tour.

Soon after his return from this journey he received the unwelcome news that his friend and patron, Walter Fawkes, had died. He was one of what might be called the 'old school' of collectors, landed gentlemen who came to admire and befriend the artists whom they patronised. Collectors of a new kind soon came to take their place as the purchasers of Turner's art, the self-made industrialists who were even then changing the entire landscape of England. Turner never returned to Farnley Hall and in a letter written a few weeks after Fawkes's death he laments that 'my good Auld lang sine is gone . . . and I must follow; indeed, I feel as you say, nearer a million times the brink of eternity'.

There was more domestic unsettlement in this period, too, and as he said 'Daddy being now released from farming thinks of feeding . . .' By which he meant that he had sold Sandycombe Lodge, thus sparing the old man the labour of gardening; the odd couple now moved into Queen Anne Street as their permanent home. But his father was now entering his eighties, a great age for a Londoner, and was clearly declining. Indeed Turner had to cancel some of his lectures on perspective, at the beginning of the following year, when his father became ill.

In the spring of 1826 Turner exhibited *Cologne* at the Royal Academy, but the canvas was noted chiefly for the artist's use of yellow. The true merits of the work went largely undiscussed. It was also reported that the controversial painting was so egregiously yellow that two adjacent portraits by Sir Thomas Lawrence seemed insipid in contrast; Turner is then supposed to have covered his canvas with a layer of lampblack to dull the resplendent effect. The tale is almost certainly apocryphal; it is unlikely that Turner would ruin the surface of one of his paintings for the sake of a fellow artist. There may be more truth in the report that

Turner had 'toned' the oil-painting with water-colour on the day preceding the exhibition. It had in fact now become part of his practice to mingle the two kinds of paint. In the same exhibition he showed *Forum Romanum for Mr Soane's Museum*, a result of his visit to Italy seven years before. Some ideas, and ideals, lingered; they waited in the wings, as it were, for the right moment of inspiration.

In this year, too, Turner was working upon what was conceived to be the largest series of engravings from his works, entitled *Picturesque Views in England and Wales*. He had agreed to provide 120 drawings, which would then be issued in 'parts' with accompanying text – four engravings in each part – and three numbers duly appeared in 1827. It was

Caricature of Turner slathering on his favourite chrome yellow. He was said to have made last-minute adjustments to one canvas by spitting on it and then using his fingers to rub in some snuff, while his painting of Jessica from *The Merchant of Venice* was nicknamed 'lady getting out of a large mustard-pot'.

essentially to furnish material for further drawings that in the same year he embarked on a number of visits to various parts of England – to Margate, to Petworth and to the Isle of Wight. On the island he was the guest of John Nash, the architect and town planner who completely changed the aspect of London with the construction of Regent Street and Regent's Park, not to mention Buckingham Palace and Trafalgar Square. He owned a castle on a hill opposite West Cowes, and from that eminence Turner proceeded to sketch views of the Cowes Regatta.

Nash also placed a painting-room at the disposal of his eminent guest, and as a result Turner stayed longer than he had expected. He was obliged to write to his father, asking him to send more painting-materials as well as extra items from his wardrobe. 'I want some Scarlet Lake and Dark Lake and Burnt Umber in powder from Newman's,' he wrote; he also needed two white waistcoats. He managed to fill three sketchbooks and began work on several paintings, some of which he worked up in time for the Royal Academy exhibition of the following year. He also completed some sketches in oil, on two different rolls of canvas. One of these works, *Study of Sea and Sky, Isle of Wight 1827*, is perhaps the first of his paintings in which he attended simply to the forces of water and cloud.

From Cowes he travelled on to Petworth, the stately home of another patron, where again he could be found hard at work in the studio provided by Lord Egremont. He rose early and worked while the other guests slept. Among the works which eventually emerged out of this disciplined routine were *Petworth Park: Tillington Church in the Distance* and *The Lake, Petworth, Sunset*. The painting of the sun setting over the lake is, in particular, an extraordinarily serene and opulent composition. A later anecdote revealed that 'when Turner painted a series of landscapes at Petworth, for the dining-room, he worked with the door locked against everybody but the master of the house'. He needed privacy and seclusion; more importantly, perhaps, he needed to know that he would not be interrupted. His host had asked him to complete some paintings to be set in the wall-panels of the dining-room, known as the Carved Room, beneath some suitably formal sixteenth-century portraits. Turner obliged, and by the summer of the following year two of them were ready for display.

Chapter Ten
1827–1833

Turner visited Margate in 1827, in part because he was suffering from ill health. It may have been thought that the sea air and the sea breeze might help to cure or at least to alleviate what seems to have been faulty breathing and a persistent cough. It should be remembered that, in London during this period, no one was ever wholly well. The smoke and fumes, as well as the miasma of vapours that rose from the river, helped to contribute to the highest mortality rate in the country. It would have been surprising if Turner had not been affected.

He came to enjoy the Margate air, and the general amenities of this seaside town. He had lived there as a child, for a short period, and it seems that he was drawn to old haunts. In his water-colours, for example, he often returned to the site of earlier work. He sketched the same scene at Knaresborough in 1797 and in 1826. He visited Norham Castle on at least three occasions – in 1797, 1801 and 1831 – as if he were testing the development of his vision.

From 1827 onward he often went down to Margate for summer weekends, either by coach or by steamer, and was once seen on the boat eating shrimps out of a handkerchief. He had more than the sea view to anticipate. One of the 'amenities' of Margate was Sophia Caroline Booth, already twice a widow (it should be remembered that Turner

enjoyed the company of Dido-like widows), who kept a
boarding-house by the promenade. They grew very close, so
close in fact that in the neighbourhood he was known as 'Mr
Booth'. After Turner's death she told an acquaintance that
'with the exception of the first year he never contributed one
shilling towards their mutual support!!!'. She was, however,
quite a wealthy widow and may have wished to retain her
financial independence. Instead he rewarded her with his
poetry, 'verses in honour of herself and her personal
charms'. Eventually he took her with him to London – to a
secret cottage in Chelsea, naturally by the river – where they
also lived as if they were man and wife.

The relationship remained unknown until after his death,
one of the many secrets lodged within the breast of this
always secretive man. One friend declared that he delighted
'in mistifying others', and this propensity may plausibly be
associated with the nature of his work itself. One family who
knew him well, the Redgraves, remarked of his paintings
that he 'ever studied to preserve a sense of *mystery*' in them.
He may not have been deliberately secretive, however; he
may have been naturally reticent, unable to discuss or reveal
those things which were closest to him. Artists in any case
are not often eloquent.

There were two paintings of Nash's castle at Cowes in the
Royal Academy exhibition of 1828, together with another
oil-painting of Dido's mythological career and a rather
strange work entitled *Boccaccio relating the Tale of the
Birdcage.* The strangeness lies in the fact that Boccaccio did
not in fact relate any tale about a bird-cage, the oddity
compounded by the fact that in the background of this

Italianate scene rises the distinctive shape of East Cowes Castle.

He was in fact eager to return to Italy again. He had regular professional work to complete, in particular the water-colours for the England and Wales series of engravings, but in the first week of August 1828 he left London for Rome. He stayed first in the south of France where the heat 'almost knocked me up'. As soon as he arrived in the Italian capital, however, he set to work. He laboured continually, beginning eight or nine pictures as well as finishing three of them. He wrote to a friend, 'but as the folk here talked that I would show them *not*, I finished a small three feet four to stop their gabbling; so now to business . . .'

His works were not always appreciated by the Italian artists, however, who according to one acquaintance of Turner's 'could make nothing of them'. When he exhibited some of his paintings in apartments in the Quattro Fontane, however, the reaction was decidedly more interesting. Among them were *Regulus* and *The Vision of Medea*, which had a wildness and extravagance of colour that astounded his contemporaries. 'You may imagine,' one English artist wrote back from Rome, 'how astonished, enraged or delighted the different schools of artists were, at seeing things with methods so new, so daring, and excellencies so unequivocal.' And that was the truth of it. His painterly techniques, indeed his whole artistic vision, was so 'new' that it was scarcely recognised or understood.

He left Rome at the beginning of 1829, and once more his coach was overturned in a snow-drift. This was either a normal occurrence on continental journeys or Turner was spectacularly unlucky with his transport. A fellow traveller left a description of him as a 'good-tempered, funny, little, elderly gentleman'. This companion did not know who Turner was but remarked that 'he is continually popping his head out of the window to sketch whatever strikes his fancy'. On one occasion the driver would not stop to take in a sunrise and Turner muttered, 'Damn the fellow! He has no feeling!' The correspondent went on to say that he 'speaks but a few words of Italian, about as much of French, which two languages he jumbles together most amusingly. His good temper, however, carries him through all his troubles. I am sure you would love him for his indefatigability in his favourite pursuit.' This testimony, from a wholly unbiased witness, suggests an almost Dickensian figure of a Cockney traveller. It is interesting that once more his amiability is stressed, in contrast to those who preferred to illustrate his less convivial qualities.

On his return to England he began to prepare for that year's exhibition at the Royal Academy, where he placed one of his favourite paintings. *Ulysses deriding Polyphemus* is also one of his most famous works. The story is out of Homer but the light and colour are from Rome. John Ruskin described it as 'the central picture in Turner's career', not least because of the visionary poetry of its conception. He has somehow managed to combine the natural and the mythological in a new synthesis, so that like one of Shakespeare's late plays we may call it a 'romance'. In the following month there was a large exhibition of his water-colours, from the England and Wales series of engravings, at the Egyptian Hall along Piccadilly.

But his delight in public recognition perhaps waned in this year, since in the autumn of 1829 his father died. William Turner had been the artist's principal confidant and friend; he had been his assistant, too, in all the business of the artist's studio and gallery. He was also his son's greatest admirer. These were impossible roles for anyone else to fill, and there is no doubt that Turner suffered a grievous blow from his father's death. After the funeral and burial in St Paul's Church in Covent Garden – where Turner was baptised and where his parents were married – he sought refuge with some old friends of the family. It was said by them that he was 'fearfully out of spirits' and confessed that it was as if he had lost an only child. This strange reversal of dependence, with the old man becoming his son, suggests an intense and overwhelming affection. The same friends noted that 'Turner never appeared the same man after his father's death; his family was broken up'. Truly he felt himself to be alone in the world, despite the comforting presence of Mrs Booth, and sensed above him the shadow of death itself.

Immediately after his father's funeral he signed his last will and testament. He left sums to his relatives, as well as annuities to Sarah and Hannah Danby; he also made bequests to the Royal Academy. He was anxious that his name should be preserved after his death, and so made arrangements for the inauguration of a Turner gold medal to be awarded every two years. The rest of his estate was left for a 'College or Charity' devoted to the care of 'decayed English artists'. He also left two paintings to the National Gallery, *Dido building Carthage* and *The Decline of the Carthaginian Empire*, on condition that they were hung perpetually between two landscapes of Claude. He changed his will on many occasions, as if he was preoccupied both with his legacy and with his posthumous fame. In a version prepared two years later he left funds for the maintenance of the gallery in Queen Anne Street 'concurring with the object of keeping my works together'. The preservation of the collection became of paramount importance to him. He was used to calling it his 'family' and he did not wish it to be dispersed. He wanted his achievement to be seen steadily and as a whole. For that reason he began to buy up examples of his earlier work when they appeared at auction. But there was also an element of self-assertion in this, amounting almost to innocence. In another version of his will he left one thousand pounds for a monument to himself in St Paul's Cathedral. This act of bravura suggests that he was not at all sure of the continuance of his fame after his demise.

Soon after his father's death Turner began work on a painting that seems to embody and reflect his mood of desolation. *Calais Sands, Low Water* is a painting of fisher-women collecting bait in the wet sand; they are all bowed low, as if in mourning, as the sun sets over the quiet waters. It was exhibited at the Royal Academy in the spring of 1830, and he would continue to hang work in that place until the year before his death; he rarely missed a season, and had become himself something of a monument within the institution. Of course many anecdotes about him now circulated among the other members, particularly concerning his behaviour on 'varnishing days'. These were the days when artists were allowed to put the finishing touches to their paintings hanging upon the walls. There was often rivalry, albeit unspoken and unacknowledged, between various artists in their search for immediate attention.

On one occasion Constable and Turner had paintings next to one another. Constable was busy adding lake and vermilion to his scene. Turner walked up, and looked from one painting to the other. Then he brought in his palette 'and putting a round daub of red lead, somewhat bigger than a shilling, on his grey sea, went away without saying a word'. Of course the bright lead made Constable's colours weaker in comparison. Another artist happened to come into the room and Constable complained to him that 'He has been here, and fired a gun.' At the last minute Turner took up his brush and turned the red spot into a buoy. On another occasion the artist David Roberts remonstrated with him for adding so much blue to his sky that his own painting looked dim in contrast. 'You attend to your business,' Turner replied, 'and leave me to attend to mine.'

This pugnacious, or competitive, quality was also evinced in disputes about the hanging of his paintings. Every artist of course wished to make sure that his work was seen to the best advantage and in the best light. Constable was on the hanging committee, one year, and aroused Turner's ire by removing a painting by Turner and replacing it with one of his own. They both attended a reception soon after this unfortunate incident and, according to one observer, 'Turner was down upon him like a sledge-hammer; it was no use his endeavour to persuade Turner that the change was for his advantage, and not his own. Turner kept at it all the evening, to the great amusement of the party . . .' Another account explained that 'Turner opened on him like a ferret; it was evident to all present Turner detested him . . . I must say that Constable looked to me and I believe to everyone else, like a detested criminal, and I must add Turner slew him without remorse.'

There were many occasions when he sent in unfinished canvases that he would then 'work up' with brush and knife (and fingers) on the spot. On one occasion, in fact, he completed an entire work on panel while it was hanging on the walls of the Academy. He would arrive early in the morning and work continually, for hours on end, never stopping to look at anyone or anything else. He would work inches from the canvas, and never once needed to step back to see the overall effect. Farington was told how he had been seen 'to *spit* all over his picture, and, then taking out a box of *brown powder*, rubbed it over the picture'. The brown powder was undoubtedly snuff. Sometimes he would stand upon a wooden box to gain the requisite height for the work. And he always wore an old, tall beaver hat. He was of course a great object then for attention and whispered comment. 'What is that he is plastering the picture with?' one artist asked another. 'I should be sorry', came the reply, 'to be the man to ask him.' When he had completed his work he shut up his box of paints and walked away without giving his finished canvas another glance. He said nothing, and left the Academy quickly. 'There, that's masterly,' the artist Daniel Maclise commented, 'he does not stop to look at his work; he knows it is done, and he is off.' A fellow artist described him in his hat and black dress-coat, with large wrappers around his head and his throat which sometimes dangled into the palette of paints. 'This, together with his ruddy face, his rollicking eye, and his continuous, although, except to himself, unintelligible jokes, gave him the appearance of that now wholly extinct race – a long-stage coachman.'

There were occasions when he volunteered practical advice to his colleagues. He said once to Maclise, who was working beside him, 'I wish, Maclise, that you would alter the lamb in the foreground, but you won't.' Maclise did as requested. 'It is better,' Turner said, 'but not right.' Whereupon he took the artist's brush and made the alteration – with which Maclise agreed. On another occasion he added some colour to a canvas by Sidney Cooper whereupon Cooper was told 'Don't touch it again – he has done in a moment all that it wanted.' Cooper went up to Turner in order to thank him, 'whereupon he nodded, and gave a sort of grunt, but vouchsafed never a word'. He seemed to be able to tell at a glance what was wrong with any picture. He walked past a canvas entitled *Squally Day* and said to the artist, of a small horse in the composition, 'You have got him turned the wrong way.' To an artist who had depicted a farmhouse in flames he muttered, as he passed, 'Put more fire in your house.'

Of his exhibits in the spring of 1830 *Calais Sands, Low Water* is perhaps the most memorable. But at the time it provoked much less comment than *Jessica*, a flaming portrait of the character in Shakespeare's *The Merchant of Venice*. The yellow background of the painting caused consternation among the public and the critics alike. It has been suggested that Turner painted it as an experiment, just to see if it could be done, but his daring earned him a great deal of abuse. When Wordsworth saw it he said that 'it looks to me as if the painter had indulged in raw liver until he was very unwell'. The theme of jaundice appeared on more than one occasion. The critic in the *Morning Chronicle* declared that 'it looks like a lady getting out of a large mustard-pot', and another artist noted that the work was 'roundabout proof that Turner was a great man; for it seems to me that none but a great man would have dared paint anything so bad'.

Jessica, or 'The Mustard Pot' as it became known, found its place in Lord Egremont's collection at Petworth. Indeed for Turner after the death of his father, as well as the death of Walter Fawkes, that stately home often became a refuge from the London world. There are a series of landscapes, as well as a number of luminous interiors, that testify to the depth of his affection for the place and for its master. The affection was reciprocated and the earl of Egremont came to possess fifteen of Turner's oil-paintings.

Turner travelled in the summer months of 1830 and 1831. In 1830 he journeyed extensively through the Midlands to find subjects for the water-colours which would become the engravings in the series entitled *England and Wales*. In the following year he travelled to Scotland, having accepted the invitation to illustrate a new edition of Scott's *Poetical Works*. The publishers knew that his illustrations would improve the sale of the collected poems immeasurably, but Turner seemed at first reluctant to undertake the commission. He and Scott had not enjoyed each other's company on a previous visit to Scotland (see p. 92). In the end he agreed and wrote to Scott asking him 'how long do you think it will take me to collect the materials in your neighbourhood'. It was a very business-like letter; there was no mention of the great honour of being in the company of

the illustrious writer, and all the other compliments conventional on such an occasion. No doubt he considered that
he was honouring Scott with his presence. Scott had in fact
only a short time to live but he seems to have been a
companionable host at Abbotsford; he and Turner would
set off on expeditions to inspect the local scenery, for which
Scott provided an appropriate historical commentary.

He did not accompany Turner to Fingal's Cave, however,
which the artist visited on what was for him a typically
stormy and rain-driven day. 'After scrambling over the rocks
on the lee side of the island,' he wrote later, 'some got into
Fingal's cave, others would not. It is not very pleasant or safe
when the wave rolls right in.' He was one of those who did
manage to enter the cavern, of course, for he sketched its
interior. He never bowed to the fury of the elements when
he anticipated a new scene or prospect opening out before
him. He completed other water-colours of the Scottish landscape, of lochs and mountains; there are great vigour and
energy in the execution, great majesty in the composition.

In the exhibition of 1832 he displayed *Staffa, Fingal's
Cave*, a wonderful composition of sea and smoke and storm
in which the varying lights of the sky and water are given
physical depth and texture; it is like some symphony of mist.
It was greatly praised by the critics, one of whom described
its 'sublimity of vastness and solitude'. It was not purchased
for another thirteen years, however, and the buyer was
reported to have said that it was 'indistinct'. Turner's reply
has been the object of much speculation. He either said
'Indistinctness is my fault' or 'indistinctness is my forte'.
Whatever the interpretation, indistinctness is certainly the
key. It may also help to describe another painting that he

placed on exhibition in this year, *Shadrach, Meshach and Abednego in the Burning Fiery Furnace.* He seems to have been inspired to paint this scene from the Book of Daniel in friendly rivalry with another artist, who had told him of his intention of depicting the biblical scene. 'A good subject,' he had said. 'I will paint it also.' It is a scene of indistinct figures and turbid fire, dismissed by one critic as one of his 'unintelligible pieces of insanity'. The painting was considered to possess a 'scorching' glare, and it was speculated that the canvas was made of asbestos – a tribute, perhaps, to the vivid immediacy of Turner's colours.

Chapter Eleven
1833–1844

In 1833 he exhibited two paintings of Venice, *Ducal Palace, Venice* and, most impressively, *Bridge of Sighs, Ducal Palace and Custom House, Venice; Canaletti painting*. This work was executed in homage to Canaletto, who is indeed seen painting the scene in the left-hand corner, but the critics seemed to agree that it was superior to the Italian artist's own paintings of his native city. The light, reflecting from an azure sky on to the calm surface of the water, was considered to be incomparable. This was in fact the first occasion when Turner had exhibited oil-paintings of Venice but he must already have known that he had chosen a highly appropriate and amenable subject. Even before the exhibition had closed, he was travelling back to that city after an absence of fourteen years. His introduction of Canaletto into his composition may also have been an indication that he wished to compete with the Italian artist on Canaletto's own ground.

He arrived in Venice at the beginning of September, having previously travelled to Vienna and Verona, and then spent little over a week there. He managed to work quickly, however, and completed some two hundred sketches in pencil. He had a way of snatching at impressions, noting in a flash what was necessary or significant, before moving on. He had a nervous dread of wasting time, and must have considered that he needed only to refresh his visual memory after the first visit.

On his return he completed *Venice* which was exhibited in the exhibition of 1834. It is perhaps significant that he charged £350 for this work, as compared with two hundred guineas for the Canaletto painting. When that had sold he had said, 'Well if they will have such scraps instead of important pictures they must pay for them.'

Some works of his were evidently not selling, and Turner considered that the 'important pictures' were those consigned to his gallery. The 'scraps' were those works which found purchasers. There was a definite sense, in other words, in which he felt himself to be estranged from public taste. He was obliged to paint only for himself, according to his own preoccupations and perceptions, and accept the fact that his productions would be looked upon with incomprehension or disfavour by the general world. He was in advance of the taste of his time, but it might have seemed appropriate to him that he would only be fully appreciated and understood by subsequent generations. He might even be seen as a forerunner of the 'modern movement' in art, in the role of Cezanne or Van Gogh, treading his own lonely path.

This romantic picture is only slightly altered by the fact that he was acquiring new patrons in this period. With the death of supporters such as Fawkes, his clients came less from the members of the aristocracy than the serried ranks of commerce. Fifty of his water-colours were purchased by a Bishopsgate coach-maker, Benjamin Windus, who exhibited them at his house in Tottenham. Among other patrons were a horse-dealer, a whaling tycoon, a textile magnate, a

John Ruskin was 21 in 1840 when he first met the 65-year-old Turner. The young man became the champion of the older artist, continuing to defend his reputation even after his death. Turner neglected to leave Ruskin any of his paintings, but in his Will named him as one of his executors, so that he could implement Turner's wish to leave his work to the nation.

Ruskin's silhouette of Turner dressed to visit the Royal Academy.

clothing manufacturer and a brewer by the name of William Whitbread. Turner appreciated commercial acumen and financial success, so he would not have been at all averse to the new owners of his work. His most vociferous supporter, John Ruskin, was after all the son of a sherry merchant. Turner was also greatly in demand from publishers who knew that his contributions to a text could help increase sales. He illustrated the work of Byron and Scott as well as such minor luminaries as Samuel Rogers and Thomas Moore.

And so he hired an agent to protect his interests. There was a time when he thought that he could supervise such matters for himself, but increasing age – as well as increasing fame – meant that he had neither the time nor the inclination. The commercial ramifications of the engraving work, for example, had become very complicated indeed. So Thomas Griffith of Norwood became his representative. Griffith was himself a collector, with an unrivalled knowledge and appreciation of contemporary art, and quickly their acquaintance changed into friendship. Another artist declared that Griffith behaved 'like a prince' in all his dealings; this was exactly the dealer that Turner now needed.

At the Royal Academy exhibition in this year, 1834, he exhibited five oils, among them *The Fountain of Indolence* and *The Golden Bough*. He was still possessed by a visionary imagination, and saw in the classical world intimations of immortal splendour. Alas the painting itself of the legendary bough was not immortal. The purchaser discovered that one of the figures was coming away from the surface of the canvas. He called in Turner who, on seeing this, exclaimed,

'Why, this is only paper!' It seems that he had made a sketch of a nude figure at the Life class of the Royal Academy and, noting that it was the right size and proportion, had simply pasted it on the painting. He had intended to paint the figure properly when it was hanging at the Exhibition 'but I forgot this entirely, and do not think I should have remembered but for you'. This was the only apology the purchaser received.

He travelled to Oxford and Brussels in the summer of 1824, once more in search of subjects for the engraver, but in fact one of his greatest themes was much closer to home. On the evening of 16 October a fire broke out in the old buildings of the Houses of Parliament, leading quickly to a general conflagration which was enjoyed by the crowds of Londoners who assembled on the banks and the bridges of the Thames. Turner was there, too, feasting on these scenes of flame and destruction. He made sketches at the time, from Westminster Bridge and Waterloo Bridge. In his studio he worked these up into two separate oil-paintings. He used the report in *The Times* for some general effects. When *The Burning of the House of Lords and Commons* was exhibited at the British Institution in the spring of 1835, however, it was praised not for its fidelity but for its magnificence. It was a visionary scene of glorious incandescence. Turner then exhibited the second painting at the Royal Academy in the same year, a painting in which a flaming sheet of fire billows across the canvas. The critic of the *Morning Chronicle* observed that 'the Academy ought, now and then, at least, to throw a wet blanket or some such damper over either this fire King or his works . . .' But

Turner was an elemental artist; fire, and water, and air, were his divinities.

He had by now become an inveterate traveller, and in the spring of 1836 he sailed from Dover to Calais for a painting trip through France. He took a companion, H.A.J. Munro, a Scottish landowner and amateur painter with whom Turner sensed an affinity. Munro recalled later how 'wherever he could get a few minutes, he had his little sketch book out, many being remarkable, but he seemed to tire at last and got careless and slovenly'. But he was not careless on his friend's behalf. Turner realised that Munro was having trouble with the colouring of his sketches. He said 'in a grumbling way – "I haven't got any paper I like; let me try yours"'. He worked on it for an hour and a half and then returned the sketchbook, saying, 'I can't make anything of your paper.' In fact he had gone through his friend's work, and cleared up every difficulty of colouring.

The anecdote was recorded in the last volume of Ruskin's *Modern Painters*, and it was in fact during this year that the then young critic emerged as Turner's most eloquent and knowledgeable supporter. Turner had exhibited at this year's Academy exhibition three paintings; they were entitled *Juliet and Her Nurse, Rome from Mount Aventine* and *Mercury and Argus*. They then became the object of a vitriolic attack in *Blackwood's Magazine*, in which an anonymous reviewer described them variously as 'a strange jumble', 'absurdities', 'a most unpleasant mixture' and altogether 'childish'. Ruskin, then only seventeen but already gifted with a preternatural alertness to art akin to genius, was enraged by the criticisms. He drafted a reply, and sent a copy of it to Turner himself. Turner thanked him for the 'zeal, kindness and the trouble you have taken in my behalf' but added that 'I never move in these matters'. He pretended never to notice criticism, in other words, and dismissed the article as of 'no import'.

Yet the young man and the old artist had forged an association which would last long after Turner's own death. Ruskin became the principal advocate of Turner's art, and it can be said with some certainty that no artist has ever had a more profound and articulate explicator. Turner's subsequent reputation, in fact, owes not a little to Ruskin's persistent and clamant advocacy. Turner professed himself unmoved by the young man's attentions. 'Have you read *Ruskin on me*?' he asked one admirer. 'He sees *more* in my pictures than I ever intended.' This is the standard reply of the artist to the critic, but there can be no doubt that Turner was secretly very pleased by his admiring attention.

The artist and his young disciple did not actually meet until a later date. It seems that on this occasion Turner scarcely noticed Ruskin at all, but the young man was keenly observant. He wrote, that evening, in his diary that

> everybody had described him to me as coarse, boorish, unintellectual, vulgar. This I knew to be impossible. I found in him a somewhat eccentric, keen-mannered, matter-of-fact, English-minded gentleman: good-natured evidently, bad-tempered evidently, hating humbug of all sorts, shrewd, perhaps a little selfish, highly intellectual, the powers of his mind not brought out with any delight in their manifestation, or intention of dis-

play, but flashing out occasionally in a word or look.

It is probably the best short description of Turner ever written.

By 1837 Turner was suffering from bad health; he was now in his early sixties, and at an age when the human body of the nineteenth century seemed to run down. In March he complained that he had 'the baneful effects of the *Influenza* hanging upon me' and confessed that 'the lassitude the sinking down and yet compelled to work the same is not to be expressed'. Here he touches upon his compulsion to work, even in the most trying circumstances, which was so integral a part of his nature. In this period, too, old friends were dying around him. W.F. Wells died, and reduced Turner to a paroxysm of sorrow. Clara Wells wrote that 'He came immediately to my house in an agony of grief. Sobbing like a child, he said, "Oh Clara, Clara! These are iron tears. I have lost the best friend I ever had in my life." ' She added 'what a different man would Turner have been if all the good and kindly feelings of his great mind had been called into action; but they lay dormant, and were known to so very few'. Lord Egremont died that winter, and of course Turner attended the funeral of his great benefactor. But by the end of that year he called himself 'an invalid and Sufferer' who could not stir out of doors. The world was beginning to wear him down. He felt further aggrieved in this year, when a number of eminent artists were knighted but he, arguably the most eminent of them all, was left out of the list.

His pre-eminence had already been proved in the spring of this year, when he prepared four large canvases for exhibition in the new galleries of the Royal Academy. They were to be opened by the king, and so an especial display of painting was desired. Turner produced *The Grand Canal, Venice* and *Snow Storm, Avalanche and Inundation* but reserved his truly grand manner for two depictions of classical subjects – *The Story of Apollo and Daphne* and *The Parting of Hero and Leander*. His technique in these works was compared to the great violinist Paganini, 'something which no one ever did or will do the like', and in particular his range of prismatic colours was admired. The quality of his light was unequalled, but it went largely without remark.

He was in fact now dwelling in his own realm of radiance, where few people could reach him. He was also moving effortlessly between the past and the present, in that enchanted space where his vision could encompass alternative realities. In the following year, 1838, he exhibited a painting entitled *Modern Italy – the Pifferari* with a companion piece entitled *Ancient Italy – Ovid Banished from Rome*. Any number of interpretations have been offered on the theme and composition of these paintings but, as always, Turner preferred to leave the spectator in a state of quickened mystery as to what, if any, ultimate meaning was to be granted to them.

At the beginning of this year he resigned his post as Professor of Perspective, a resignation that was no doubt received without regret by the members of the Academy; he had been dilatory and surprisingly unprofessional in his discharge of these duties. It had become a burden rather than an honour.

It may have been with some fellow-feeling, then, that he watched a warship, the *Téméraire*, being towed by small tugs to a ship-breaking yard at Rotherhithe. Some friends say that he watched the spectacle while returning on the packet-steamer from Margate, a sure indication that his relationship with Mrs Booth was still satisfactory. Other friends, however, believe that he was returning from a day trip to Greenwich when he observed the arresting sight of this grand vessel being towed along the Thames to her last destination.

The Fighting Téméraire has become one of his most famous paintings. When it was exhibited at the Royal Academy in 1839 it was greeted with universal acclaim, and did much to erase the unsatisfactory impression his most recent canvases had produced. It was regarded as a work of genius, and for John Ruskin it became 'the last thoroughly perfect picture [he] ever painted'. William Makepeace Thackeray called it 'as grand a painting as ever figured on the walls of any academy, or came from the easel of any painter'. Further comment is perhaps superfluous except to note that Thackeray expressed regret that there was no 'art of translating colours into music or poetry'. That is the secret of *The Fighting Téméraire*: the art of colour itself is taken to the highest possible pitch. It is deployed, like music or the language of poetry, for its own sake without any recourse to some ultimate reality. The light is not of this earth but has the effulgence of a vision.

There is some dispute over whether Turner is depicting a sunrise or a sunset, but in this context it does not matter. He never sold the painting and it was found among his effects after his death.

He was on his travels again in 1839, and revisited the three rivers that he had explored before – the Rhine, the Meuse and the Mosel. He seems to have remained an eager and indefatigable traveller, and on this extended painting expedition he sketched most of the notable cities and towns along his route.

He still relished his trips on the continent – 'on the Wing', as he put it – and from 1841 he journeyed to Switzerland over four successive years. He travelled along the Rhine on each occasion and, remarkably, tended to reproduce the scenes and images that he had captured on his first journey in 1817.

In these years, too, he continued exhibiting at the Royal Academy. He displayed no less than six canvases in 1840, among them the controversial *Slavers throwing overboard the Dead and the Dying – Typhoon coming on,* a painting of great turbulence, with the masses of water and air billowing out into the most vivid colours. It is as if the sea and the sky had become thrones of blood. Ruskin declared that 'if I were reduced to rest Turner's immortality upon any single work, I should choose this', although the more conventional critics reacted with the usual horror to the artist's 'absurdities'. He was in fact now becoming the subject of popular satire. The humorous magazine, *Punch,* invented a catalogue entry which included 'A Typhoon bursting   in a simoon over the Whirlpool of Maelstrom, Norway, with a Ship on fire, an Eclipse, and the Effect of a Lunar Rainbow'. In a London pantomime of 1841 there was a scene in which a boy with a tray of jam tarts falls through a window in which a Turner painting is being displayed; the shop owner dusts down the broken tarts, puts a frame around them, and sells them for a thousand pounds.

There is one anecdote, again from Ruskin, that suggests something of the artist's temperament. Turner was sitting at dinner, almost directly opposite his painting of the slave-ship, and throughout the meal 'his eyes never turned to it'. He ignored one of his greatest creations. It was a question of reticence and self-restraint.

But he had truly become the most famous artist of his day. Certainly he seems to have sensed the full power of his achievement. The figures are in themselves impressive. In the four years 1841 to 1844, he exhibited no less than twenty-three large oil-paintings. This was a high rate of productivity, even by his standards, but the steady flow of composition in no way impeded his mastery. He relished labour, too, and used to repeat the same confession that 'The only secret I have got is damned hard work' com-plemented by 'I know of no genius but the genius of hard work'.

Among the labour of these years emerge some of his finest paintings, among them *Rain, Steam and Speed – the Great Western Railway* and *Snow Storm*. The latter painting had probably the longest, and certainly the most eccentric, title ever recorded in the catalogue of the Royal Academy – *Steam Boat off a Harbour's Mouth making Signals in Shallow Water, and going by the Lead. The Author was in this storm on the Night the Ariel left Harwich.* Turner always insisted that he had been involved in the entire incident. One acquaintance reported him as saying, 'I did not paint to be understood, but I wished to show what such a scene was like; I got the sailors to lash me to the mast to observe it; I was lashed for four hours, and I did not expect to escape, but I felt bound to record it if I did. But no one had any business to like the picture.' It all sounds a little too extraordinary to be true but the painting itself is worth all of his putative endeavours, with the ship in the middle of a great funnel of charged forces. The picture evoked the usual reactions. One critic described it as 'soapsuds and white-wash', to which Turner was heard to respond: 'Soapsuds and whitewash! What would they have? I wonder what they think the sea's like? I wish they'd been in it.'

Rain, Steam and Speed is a token for Turner's experiments in colour during this period, an exercise in what may be called the vaporous sublime, in which the material world is wreathed in a veil of majesty and in which the laying down of pure colour elicits the most powerful and profound responses. He was trying to create a new sense of form as an inalienable property of light.

His late paintings were not in any case meant to be immediately comprehended. When Ruskin said to him that 'the worst of his pictures was that one could never see enough of them', he replied, 'That's part of their quality.'

Chapter Twelve
1844–1851

By the mid-1840s, Turner was significantly ageing. He wrote to a friend that 'the evening beat me. Time always hangs hard upon me, but his auxiliary, Dark weather, has put me quite into the background, altho' before Xmas I conceived myself in advance of Mr Time.' In 1846 he seems finally to have abandoned domestic life in Queen Anne Street and left the house and gallery there to the attentions of Hannah Danby whom, in letters, he had a habit of calling 'my damsel', although anyone looking less like a 'damsel' would be hard to imagine. He moved to a small house in Cremorne Road, Chelsea, just by a bend in the river. He constructed a kind of gallery on the roof of this building, and from there he could sit and watch the changing light upon the river. It is said by one who knew him well that he would climb the stairs on to the roof before sunrise 'and if there was a fair promise of an effective rising he would remain to study it, making pencil notes of the form of clouds, and writing in brief their tints of colour'.

The place had another attraction also. Sophia Booth shared the house with him, and indeed they lived together for all practical purposes as man and wife. She claimed that she had paid for the lease, with 'Turner refusing to give a farthing towards it'. There are many anecdotes of their life here, gathered from Mrs Booth herself and from the neighbours who were alternately amused and mystified by Turner's odd behaviour. It seems that he was known to the locals as 'Admiral Booth' or 'Puggy Booth', no doubt because of his whimsical nautical appearance. Turner called Mrs Booth 'Old 'un', like a character out of Dickens, and she knew him as 'dear'. 'There are times,' Sophia told a picture-dealer, 'when I feel he must be a god.' It was rumoured in the locality that he was a great man in disguise, and that on his death he would be buried in St Paul's Cathedral, but no one knew the actual truth of the matter. He was said to sit by himself in a local public house, and indeed there are stories of his excessive drinking towards the end of his life. But he still retained his reputation for secrecy and mystery. He was seen by an artist in the Chelsea pub one rainy evening, and the acquaintance said to him, 'I shall often drop in now I've found out where you quarter.' 'Will you,' Turner replied. 'I don't think you will.' Whereupon he finished his drink and left.

He was more convivial in less private circumstances. He had become a founder member of the Athenaeum in 1824, for example, and in these latter years 'was always to be seen between ten and eleven at the Athenaeum, discussing his half-pint of sherry. As his health failed, he became very talkative after his wine and rather dogmatic.' He could also become triumphant after two or three drinks. When he was with Walter Fawkes's son, Hawksworth, in a London hotel he staggered around saying, 'I am the real lion. I am the great lion of the day, Hawkey.' When a young artist observed him in 1847 he reported that there is no evidence of unhealthy biliousness in his face. It is red and full of living blood, and although age has left its mark on him it does not seem to have taken the energy of his mind, for that lives in the observant eye and that compressed mouth, the evidence of an acute, penetrating intellect, which I may mention is seen in the whole contour of his face. He is a great little man – and all acknowledge it.

This great little man was able to provide six canvases for the Royal Academy exhibition of 1846, but in the following year he produced only one – and that itself was a worked-over version of a canvas he had stored in his gallery. In truth he could not work because he was no longer in good health. It seems that he was obliged to forfeit all his teeth as a result of some disease or disorder of the gums. A dentist constructed a set of false ones but they were not altogether successful; as a result his digestion was impaired and his health weakened. He could only suck solid foods, and therefore became more reliant upon drink of every sort. He was placed on a diet of rum and milk, which he would drink to excess. And of course he may have taken alcohol in other forms to help curb the continual pain that he seemed to endure.

The dentist, W. Bartlett – who was also a 'surgeon' and a 'cupper' or blood-letter – explained later that he visited the little house in Cremorne Road three or four times each day during Turner's illness, and reported that 'there was nothing about the house to indicate the abode of an artist. The *Art Journal* and the *Illustrated London News* were always on the table. He was very fond of smoking and yet had a great objection to any one knowing of it.' The artist told Bartlett that, if he recovered, he would 'take me on the continent and show me all the places he had visited'.

But he fell ill again, and Mrs Booth took him down to Margate in order to savour the sea air. He then suffered from some kind of fit at Rochester. In the following year he seems to have contracted cholera, in one of those virulent epidemics that swept over London in the mid-nineteenth century. Areas like Cremorne Road, close to the effluent of the river, were particularly affected. But somehow or other he survived. Mrs Booth's nursing must have had a beneficial effect; she was 'most unwearied, being up night and day'. But his own hardy constitution played a part in his recovery. He was tough and durable.

Despite his bouts of severe ill health he had not lost his curiosity. He was particularly interested in the new invention of photography and, unlike many of his artistic contemporaries, did not consider the production of the daguerreotype to be any kind of threat to genuine painting. He knew well enough that an artist did much more than merely record impressions. In the late 1840s Turner used to visit a photographic shop in the Strand run by a Mr Mayall. The proprietor knew nothing of his visitor, except that he believed him to be a 'Master in Chancery'. How he received that impression is not clear.

Mayall took several daguerreotypes of Turner and stated later that 'I recollect one of these portraits was presented to the lady who accompanied him'. The gift was no doubt presented to Mrs Booth. On one visit the artist 'stayed for some three hours, talking about light and its curious effects on films of prepared silver. He expressed a wish to see the spectral image copied.'

So Turner had not lost his enthusiasm for the effects of light. It had in fact remained his central preoccupation. He was 'always with some new notion about light' on subsequent visits, and was particularly interested in Mayall's photographs of the Niagara Falls. He 'inquired of me about the effect of the rainbow spanning the great falls'. Mayall had a plate of that phenomenon, which Turner wished to buy. But it was not to be sold. It was too singular. Mayall recalled that he was inquisitive and observant, curious about every aspect of his work. It was for Turner, after all, a new pictorial world.

It was only later, when he met his visitor at a soirée of the Royal Society, that Mayall was informed he knew '*the* Mr Turner'. Turner carried on chatting about the spectrum as if nothing whatever had been said. If it seems somewhat odd that Mayall had taken him for a legal figure, it may have been the impression that Turner wished to leave. There is the story of his putting on the Lord Chancellor's wig, at a private supper, where he was 'so joyous and happy . . . in the idea that the Chancellor's wig became him better than any one else of the party'. A legal persona, like the marine persona, may have suited him.

In 1847 or 1848 he opened a drawing-book which Ruskin later called Turner's 'Actually Last Sketchbook'. There are only a few drawings within it. He exhibited no work at the Royal Academy in 1848, only the fourth time in fifty-eight years that he had nothing on display in that institution. But in this same year a painting of his was placed in the National Gallery; his *The Dogana, San Giorgio, Citella, from the steps of the Europa* was thus among the Old Masters whom he so revered, and has the distinction of being the first Turner ever displayed in that place. It was transferred to the Tate Gallery, the formal home of Turner's painting, in 1949.

It may have been this recognition by the national collection that persuaded him to change his will in 1848. He left his finished pictures to the National Gallery 'provided that a room or rooms are added to the present National Gallery to be when erected called "Turner's Gallery" in which such pictures are to be constantly kept deposited and preserved'. If these provisions were not met, the paintings were to remain in Queen Anne Street.

In the following year he seems to have been working upon what may justly be called his last paintings. He reworked a canvas that he had completed some forty years before, *The Wreck Buoy*, but he concentrated principally upon the sky that is irradiated by a double rainbow. He was also working on four new canvases, once more exploring the myth of Dido and Aeneas that had haunted him for so many years. It seems that he painted them in a row, going from one to the other in his familiar fashion. There were also some ten unfinished paintings that date from the last years of his life; whether they were unfinished as a result of age or weariness, or whether they had been left in that state to be reworked on the varnishing days of the exhibition, is an open question.

In the Christmas of 1849 he wrote to Hawksworth Fawkes saying that 'I am sorry to say my health is on the wain. I cannot bear the same fatigue, or have the same bearing against it I formerly had – but time and tide stop not.' He was now in his seventy-fifth year. There were many, however, who saw no lack of mastery in the last works he exhibited. When the paintings of Aeneas were shown at the Royal Academy in the spring of 1850 a friend wrote that 'your intellect defies time to injure it, and I really believe that you never conceived more beautiful, more graceful, or more enchanting compositions'.

One of the last descriptions of Turner dates from this year, when a young American encountered him in his gallery in Queen Anne Street. 'I never saw a keener eye than his, and the way that he held himself up, so straight that he seemed almost to lean backwards, with his forehead thrown forward, and the piercing eyes looking out from under their heavy brows, combined to make a very peculiar and vivid impression on me.' When the American ventured to remark that his country had the good fortune to own one of Turner's 'sea-coast sunsets' the artist remarked, 'I wish they were all put in a blunderbuss and shot off!'

He was living in Cremorne Road in 1851, the last year of his life. He had told a friend that 'Old Time has made sad work with me' but he still attended dinners with friends, and on occasions made short trips along the river that he had known since his earliest childhood. He had no work to exhibit at that year's exhibition but he visited on varnishing days; at the private view that year a fellow artist believed that he 'was breaking up fast'. Yet at a party in the spring he conversed with other guests on politics and books as he had always done. One guest believed him to be 'as secure in health, as firm in tone of mind, as keen in interest, as when I had seen him years before'. But he was too ill to attend the reception at the end of the exhibition.

A friend and fellow artist, David Roberts, wrote him a letter asking to visit him. But Turner, true to his habit of secrecy, came to see Roberts instead. 'You must not ask me,' he said, 'but whenever I come to town I will always come to see you.' Then he laid his hand upon his heart and muttered, 'No, no; there is something here which is all wrong.' Yet according to Roberts his eyes were as bright and as alert as they ever were. There was a large painting upstairs in Roberts's studio, but Turner was too infirm to mount the stairs.

He was still working in Cremorne Road. Mrs Booth recalled how he would often call out for drawing materials even as he lay ill in bed. Hannah Danby, his housekeeper at Queen Anne Street, grew anxious at his absence. She found the address of Cremorne Road, and the name of Mrs Booth, in one of his coat pockets. Whereupon the poor woman travelled to the neighbourhood with a female friend for support. It seems that they were afraid to knock upon the door of the house and instead enquired about Mrs Booth in a ginger-beer shop next door. 'The answer was that two very quiet *respectable* people of that name had lived for years next door, but that the old gentleman had been very ill and in fact was supposed to be dying.' Hannah Danby left, without ever seeing her old employer.

Mrs Booth again took him to Margate for a change of air but, once there, he insisted on returning to London. It may be that he wished to die in the only place he truly loved. A doctor visited him there, and told him that death was coming soon. 'Go downstairs,' Turner said, 'take a glass of sherry and then look at me again.' The doctor did so, but saw no reason to change his opinion. 'Then,' Turner said, 'I am soon to be a nonentity.'

He died a few days later, on the morning of 19 December. An hour before his death the sun burst through the gloomy clouds. A few weeks earlier he is supposed to have remarked that 'the sun is God'. The remark may be apocryphal, but it is appropriate enough for an artist who loved the light beyond all other things. He died by the river, where he had been born.

Select Bibliography

In this series of short biographies I have not thought it appropriate to introduce footnotes and source notes within the text. Here instead is a list of sources and secondary materials that have been employed in the preparation of the narrative.

Bailey, Anthony, *Standing in the Sun. A Life of J.M.W. Turner* (London, 1997).

Bayes, Walter, *Turner: A Speculative Portrait* (London, 1931).

Butlin, Martin and Joll, Evelyn, *The Paintings of J.M.W. Turner*, two volumes (London, 1984).

Finberg, A.J., *The Life of J.M.W. Turner RA* (Oxford, 1961).

Gage, John, *Turner: 'A Wonderful Range of Mind'* (New Haven, 1987).

Hamerton, P.G., *The Life of J.M.W. Turner RA* (London, 1879).

Hamilton, James, *Turner: A Life* (London, 1997).

Hill, David, *Turner in the North* (London, 1996).

—— *Turner on the Thames* (London, 1993).

Lindsay, Jack, *Turner* (London, 1966).

Powell, Cecilia, *Turner's Rivers of Europe* (London, 1991).

Shanes, Eric, *Turner: The Great Watercolours* (London, 2000).

Townsend, Joyce, *Turner's Painting Techniques* (London, 1993).

Warrell, Ian, *Turner and Venice* (London, 2003).

Index